FIELDWORK TRAINING IN SOCIAL WORK

FIELDWORK TRAINING IN SOCIAL WORK

I.S. SUBHEDAR

RAWAT PUBLICATIONS
Jaipur • New Delhi • Bangalore • Guwahati • Kolkata

ISBN 978-81-7033-645-7

Reprinted, 2016

Published by
Prem Rawat for **Rawat Publications**
Satyam Apts., Sector 3, Jawahar Nagar, Jaipur - 302 004 (India)
Phone: 0141 265 1748 / 7006 Fax: 0141 265 1748
E-mail : info@rawatbooks.com
Website: rawatbooks.com

New Delhi Office
4858/24, Ansari Road, Daryaganj, New Delhi 110 002
Phone: 011-23263290

Also at *Bangalore, Guwahati* and *Kolkata*

Typeset by Rawat Computers, Jaipur
Printed at Nice Printing Press, New Delhi

Dedicated to by Beloved Parents
Late Shri Suleman Sahab and BiBi Jehra

Also Dedicated to my Beloved Teacher
Dr S.N. Pawar
Acting Registrar, Shivaji University, Kolhapur

Contents

	Foreword	9
	Acknowledgements	11
	Preface	13
	Introduction	17
1	Fieldwork Training	22
2	Fieldwork Supervision	39
3	Orientation Training	57
4	Work with Individuals	70
5	Work with Groups	95
6	Work with Community	117
7	Social Functions	138
8	Study Tours	145
9	Rural Social Work Camps	156
10	Fieldwork through Films	192
11	Fieldwork Evaluation	198
12	Summer Training	235
	Bibliography	272
	Index	273

Foreword

Social work education underwent climactic changes in the late 60s and early 70s after the first School of Social Work was opened in India in 1936 by Sir Dorabji Tata–today known as Tata Institute of Social Sciences, Mumbai. There have been various books on professional social work education. However, fieldwork training which is considered to be the backbone of social work has been neglected and there has been no literature available on this subject. Unfortunately, those professionally trained in the field also seem to have failed in satisfying the expectations of the communities or institutions, and the educators as well as students of social work are unable to understand how to put the theoretical knowledge learnt in schools, to practice.

It is from this point of view that I have welcomed the conscientious and sincere work of my close friend and colleague, Dr. I. S. Subhedar, who has rendered more than 20 years of service in this profession. In Volume I of this two-volume series, he has attempted to enlighten and guide the reader/student about fieldwork training in social work education. This book is the first of its kind and Dr. Subhedar has given detailed information about fieldwork training, its meaning, need, scope and application of the theoretical knowledge of social work. He has also highlighted the importance of rural camps, social functions and summer training in imparting a healthy education to the students.

In order to make the concept understandable jargon and complicated terminology have been avoided. The language has deliberately been kept simple.

I am confident that this book will be handy for teachers and useful to students of social work and also to social work practitioners. I heartily congratulate him for his pioneering effort, and wish him and the publication a grand success.

Laxmikant A. Patil
Ex Director
Walchand College of Social Work
Solapur, Maharashtra

Acknowledgements

In devising this book and shaping my views on fieldwork training a number of experts and friends have assisted me and contributed a lot directly or indirectly. It is very difficult to mention the names of all. However, a few of them are responsible for developing the creativity and directions for writing the ideas of fieldwork in this book and I will not be satisfied without mention of their names–Dr. Lakshmikant Appasaheb Patil, Secretary, Janata Shiskshan Mandal, Arjunnagar, Pattankudi; Prof. Vilas Pandurang Bet, Director, Walchand College of Social Work, Solapur; and Dr. Basavaraj Lawani, Faculty Member, Bharati Vidyapeeth's Institute of Management, Solapur. All these friends and philosophers have not just motivated me in accomplishing the target of presenting the ideas of fieldwork, but it can be said that this book is the outcome of a culmination of their practical knowledge. They have provided timely and proper guidance whenever it was required. I am indebted to them for their unforgettable and worthy contribution. Mr. Prashant Rajput, my friend, spared his valuable time to correct the sequences of the contents, for copy editing, language editing, sequencing of the book and designing the book and also motivated me to complete the writing. Without his services this book would not have come out so early. I express my deep sense of gratitude for his valuable intellectual and professional services.

I am indebted to my family members especially my youngest brother Mustaque alias Kundan Subhedar (film artist), younger sister Meharnigar, and my sons Zulfikar and Shamshoddin who motivated me to accomplish the task. I express my sincere acknowledgements to them for their encouragement and cooperation.

I wish to dedicate this work to my late parents who even sold their ornaments and property to help me complete my professional training. I also dedicate this book to my beloved teacher Prof. Dr. S.N. Pawar, Acting Registrar, Shivaji University, Kolhapur, for developing my social outlook and perspective for stimulating me in building my professional career and for understanding me during my good and bad moments.

I would highly appreciate any criticism or suggestions that would come my way in helping me to improve the quality of the book.

Iqbal Subhedar

Preface

Professional training in social work education started in India in 1936 with the establishment of Sir Dorabji Tata Graduate School of Social Work at Mumbai (today it is the Tata Institute of Social Sciences, Mumbai). Later other schools of social work came into existence under the auspices of the Christian missionaries. Universities and colleges located in different parts of the country followed and introduced similar courses in due course of time. In this way professional training in social work education has spread to all parts of the country today. Initially this training started in labour welfare and correctional administration and later on it has covered the other fields of social work like family, child and youth welfare, rural and urban development, medical and psychiatric social work, etc.

In the beginning, professional training was introduced as generic training but different specialisations developed in due course. Even today both these training methods, i.e., generic and specialised, are available in the country. In generic training a specialised theory paper and practicals are included for introductory studies. That is why both generic and specialised trained social workers are absorbed in any field of social work. Today 65 years of professional training have been imparted in India but unfortunately neither have the generic and specialised courses in social work earned professional recognition, nor do they generate professional values as is expected in the market of professional services. Besides, the pioneer institute, i.e., Tata Institute of Social Sciences Mumbai, has dropped the popular and job-oriented specialisation, viz., labour welfare and personnel management courses from its syllabus in social work and has allowed all graduates to be admitted to the course of social sciences. However, other universities have continued the specialisation of personnel management and labour welfare.

In the last six and half decades, professional training in social work education has not been developed as it should have been. In fact, it should have earned the status of an independent profession because of its specialty, i.e., concurrent fieldwork training. Fieldwork training is the back bone of social work education but unfortunately professionally trained persons seem to have failed in reaching the core of the training. Moreover, it seems that sufficient efforts have also not been made by the concerned to develop it according to the needs of the communities and also for making the students perfect in their chosen profession. Relevant and sufficient practical-oriented literature on fieldwork has not been produced either by theoreticians or by the practitioners. However, some of the theoreticians have made an attempt to elaborate the concepts, meanings, nature, scope, techniques and the skills of social work. So far in these 65 years, not a single textbook has been written on fieldwork training in social work education. The students, therefore, are unable to understand the use of social work techniques, principles and values in the actual field of practice. This is more so in the case of students of the moffussil areas. Most of the time they are confused about the modalities, i.e., how to begin fieldwork practice and how to complete it. They do not understand the nature, scope, extension and magnitude of fieldwork training. As a result of this even marginally qualified students are scarce to find in this field. Moreover, the multitude of underqualified students are also not easily absorbed in the market. Naturally, such trained professional social workers are unable to effectively solve the problems of the people in this changing society as compared to the untrained voluntary social work practitioners and field activists.

Research scholars working in the departments of social work in different universities and colleges have made an attempt to study fieldwork training in social work education and have recorded certain valuable and viable suggestions for its improvements. In spite of this, the necessary and expected change has not taken place in the nature and scope of fieldwork training. Of course, the universities and colleges located in the metropolitan cities have tried to develop the field practicum according to the needs of the communities and the changing concepts of fieldwork training in the world, but the universities and colleges located in moffussil areas have not developed it as expected in the fields. Hence, traditional fieldwork training is practised everywhere with the help of the theory syllabus. The schools and colleges have still not come out of the traditional framework of institutional training of social work techniques.

In the two-year professional course, the first year's course is general which includes all the concerned social sciences along with the theoretical social work papers, and the specialisation papers have been incorporated in the second year. In the first year's syllabus, a lot of concurrent fieldwork has been included for learning the practical aspects of social work techniques in social welfare agencies as well as in the open communities. The said fieldwork training is being completed in two phases: (i) orientation, and (ii) concurrent fieldwork. The other methods: (i) study tours, and (ii) rural camps are also used in some schools/colleges, but in general these two methods are used commonly together for the first and second year. These methods are not used to impart training according to the specialisations. Similarly, fieldwork training is not imparted systematically and scientifically due to a lack of proper infrastructure facilities and amenities, non-availability of trained persons, equipment, funds, practical syllabus, literature and manuals, etc., in moffussil areas.

Considering the shortcomings and lacunae I have made an attempt to write a book on fieldwork for the students of both the classes, i.e., MSW Part I and MSW Part II, to enable them to understand the concepts, methods, professionality, modalities, etc., and also to enable the faculty supervisors and agency supervisors guide the students in achieving the goals to make them perfect trained professional social workers. Two volumes on fieldwork training in social work education have been planned. The first volume deals with fieldwork training for first year students of Social Work and the second volume with specialised fieldwork training for second year students of Social Work.

Twenty years of practical experience in the field apart from training, discussions and research have gone into the preparations of this book. I have made an attempt to throw light on the existing training and its procedures and methods, as well as to devise modalities of doing fieldwork training and extend its scope to include summer training. The contents of summer training are:

(i) setting up voluntary organisation, and

(ii) preparing proposals for grants-in-aid, running the voluntary organisation, etc.

The second volume of this book is still incomplete and I welcome constructive suggestions from experts in the field. If found suitable they could be incorporated in the forthcoming volume.

Iqbal Subhedar

Introduction

The tradition of social service took a scientific turn with the development of social sciences and we moved from charity to self-improvement. Stress has been laid on the application of scientific methods for the diagnosis and solution of social problems by studying the socio-economic factors of problems and acquiring special skills and techniques in dealing with them.

The first school of social work was set up in Bombay in 1936, which produced social workers with professional training. Climatic changes occurred in social work and social work education during the late 1960s and early 1970s. For the first time since 1939, undergraduate social work education was officially recognised, standards were set and accreditation of undergraduate programmes by the Council for Social Work was instituted. Large numbers of students today are enrolling in social work courses.

Social work aims at creating conditions for individuals, groups and communities under which they are able to utilise their potentialities and existing resources to remove some of the handicaps and to overcome them by proper adjustment, in order to live their life more adequately and creatively.

Social work profession has developed certain methods and techniques, which have been tested and today have become areas of social work. These are:

(i) Social casework,
(ii) Social group work,
(iii) Community organisation,
(iv) Social action,
(v) Social work administration, and
(vi) Social work research.

Schools of social work offer courses in social work education, basic methods and techniques, fields of social work/welfare and fieldwork. Though schools provide theoretical background of social work profession, students are often confused about fieldwork. There is a reasonable demand to be taught something, about how social workers engage in practice and serve as agents of change, about the nature of social work intervention and its purpose, how is it carried out, and the processes through which the supervisors/ social work trainees/clients move through.

In this book an effort has been made to identify, conceptualise and organise certain common elements of social work practice, so that they can be logically and systematically examined by the student exploring the potential of an existing profession.

The book rests on the assumption that common curriculum and processes of social work and fieldwork practice can be identified, and these are applicable to student trainees, regardless of the settings, viz., correctionals, mental health, schools, public welfare, etc., or the relational systems, individuals, family, small group, community, in which they are placed for fieldwork.

As used here, the process may be defined as a series of actions, changes or functions that bring about an end result. The practical exposure will develop confidence in the students in dealing with problems of clients with the help of scientific knowledge and skills and techniques adopted through classroom teaching.

This book is an effort to combine the advantages of both theoretical information and practical training. It consists of twelve extensive chapters. The purpose of this introduction is to provide continuity and integration and to set forth the author's viewpoint.

Fieldwork is a dynamic process of creative and innovative ideas. It fosters the development of intellectual and emotional processes and attitudes. This training started as field instructions with apprenticeship in social agencies. The tasks given to the trainees were similar to those given to craftsmen and there was dichotomy between administrative and non-administrative skills. Therefore, fieldwork is considered to be learning through doing.

The first chapter narrates the development of fieldwork training and gives its objectives. It explains how important fieldwork practice is to the student. Sincere application of thought by the students on issues highlighted in the chapter will make them confident.

The second chapter deals with fieldwork supervision. It is very useful, both to the students as well as the supervisors, of schools and agencies. The importance of fieldwork supervision has been stressed in this chapter and it also provides valuable suggestions to the schools for better supervision of the fieldwork process.

The third chapter is on orientation that has to be imparted to students by the faculty and agency supervisors. Important aspects of the orientation process have been identified and presented. Various formats and model charts have been illustrated for use. It is said, "work well begun is half done." In this context orientation plays a very important part and therefore, students should read this carefully and understand all the aspects.

The fourth chapter "Work with Individuals" is specific to casework. Illustrations, model diaries, model journals and model charts have been provided to facilitate a proper recording of points. Casework is one of the most important activities any prospective social worker will carry out during his career. In this context it is very important that the students understand this chapter thoroughly.

The fifth chapter discusses working with groups. Group work, as a tool of social work, is very often misunderstood. The concepts of group work are not clear and therefore, group work as a tool of social work is seldom practised by social workers. Humans, being social animals, regulate their behaviour in relation to the expected patterns set by society. Group work helps social workers to observe and study this social behaviour and identify people whose behaviour is not in line with the patterns expected by society.

"Work with Communities", which is the sixth chapter, highlights the importance of working with communities in community settings. The most important difference in working in community settings is that the students have no compulsions or procedural bindings, as is the case when working with agencies. The communities offer the prospective social work students a free environment to put their skills to experiment. Working in a free environment does not, however, mean that there are no margins for error. Any error, either judgmental or practised, will have fatal results. The students therefore, should exercise caution. The chapter deals at length, the importance, procedures and methods of working with communities.

The seventh chapter is about social functions. Normally, all of us attend social functions. However, we seldom give any importance to them in terms of the learning opportunities they provide. In this chapter the author has made an effort to identify and discuss these opportunities, along with the objectives, methods and procedures of study in social functions.

The eighth chapter discusses study tours. Study tours are goldmines of knowledge and often mean fun. But sadly enough, they end only with the objective of fun achieved. Study tours actually are a vast source of information. They provide the students with the opportunity, not only to see social work successes but also to meet the people who made them happen. In terms of their utility as tools of learning, study tours can be compared to treasure chests. These treasures not only shine (fun) but are also very precious (learning). The points enumerated in this chapter, not only relate to the objectives but also highlight the various important procedures and learning points, and will certainly prove very useful to the students.

The ninth chapter is entitled "Rural Social Work Camps". A social work camp assists the students to understand the core of rural life, rural problems and rural needs, and helps them to prepare a social plan for social work practice and community development in future. Most often such camps are compared to the NSS camps which are organised by NSS members in colleges and schools. Prospective social work students should be careful in distinguishing these camps from those of social work camps. The author has brought out these distinguishing features and explains them in detail.

The next chapter covers fieldwork through films. As in the case of study tours, films also give infinite opportunities to prospective social workers to understand various social issues, which are brought out vividly in films. The author urges the students of social work to concentrate more on such issues and discern the social problems dealt with in the films, instead of merely watching them for entertainment purposes. Examples quoted are of use.

Chapter eleven is about fieldwork evaluation. Evaluation is the most important and feared part in a student's life. However, it is one of those things, without which life would have no meaning. It is the survival of the fittest. And there must be ways defined in deciding who is the fittest. Evaluation in fieldwork is often taken very lightly by the supervisors and the students. In fact, since proper fieldwork practices can teach students much more than theory can ever do, fieldwork evaluation should be considered with more dignity than it is being credited with today. In this chapter the author has given model evaluation sheets which will prove very useful to the faculty.

The last chapter deals with summer training. The objectives, models and specimen charts/letters given will prove very useful. The author has also discussed the importance of setting up individual NGOs. Procedures, methods and issues relating to the setting up of NGOs have been detailed. Proper understanding and implementation can prove very useful to the students in standing on their own.

All the chapters have covered in detail, the background, the objectives, the methods and procedures, alongwith the author's suggestions. Wherever necessary, model charts, formats, examples, diaries and journals have been provided.

Chapter 1

Fieldwork Training

"Fieldwork training makes the students employable and confident to face the interviews and challenges in professional practice."

Background

Social work education started in the form of apprenticeship by the Charity Organisation Society of America and was initiated to impart training in social work as a profession in the year 1898. The Charity Organisation Society started social work education for providing training to newly recruited employees. The nature of training was only practical and not theoretical. It was just a five-week programme for the practical training of the newly recruited employees. The method of training was also simple in nature, i.e., observation of the work performed by their senior employees during office hours in practical situations. There were neither theory classes conducted for the purpose, nor was there any assessment of the recruit's performance, based on theoretical understanding of the concerned field or job. Thus, social work education emerged out of practical field training. The credit goes to Mary Richmond, one of the officials in that charity organisation, for projecting the concept and ideas of social casework and social work education. She is, therefore, known as the pioneer or mother of social casework, and the organisation is considered to be the successful projector of social work education.

Concept of Fieldwork

Fieldwork in social work education refers to training and education. The training is repetitive and skill-oriented and education is imparted with broad perspectives. It consists of accumulating knowledge in different situations. It is a dynamic process of observing, amassing and implementing creative and innovative ideas. Moreover, it fosters the development of intellectual and emotional processes and attitudes. This training started as field instruction with apprenticeship in social agencies. The tasks given to trainees were similar to those given to craftsmen and there was dichotomy between administrative and non-administrative skills. Therefore, fieldwork is considered to be learning through doing. The ideas of Dewey, i.e., learning through doing has had a primary influence in the concept of fieldwork. It is an integrating factor, acting as a balancing force between the two companions of social work, which has crucial significance in the training of social work. It blends theory with practice, combines philosophy with action, integrates the understanding about people with methods of helping them. The techniques drew heavily on scientific knowledge about people and social phenomena. It is functional and technical in nature, and fosters learning in students. Moreover, it is an integrated approach, which goes concurrently with the classroom teaching process. Fieldwork programme provides an opportunity to students to apply their theoretical knowledge taught in the classroom appropriately in different practical situations. Similarly, it serves as a social laboratory, wherein a student tests his theoretical knowledge in practical situations and develops the skills for social living. It is a way to transform knowledge through certain skills and techniques into action. The significance of fieldwork training in social work is consequential because of its nature of dealing with problems practically. Mere classroom lectures are not enough to comprehend practical situations, in professional education. It was this fact which prompted Annette Garrette to write, "an extensive well planned fieldwork programme is inevitable". It becomes very important in dealing with the dynamics of the human personality in the context of an individual's needs. It is evident that fieldwork varies in quality and quantity. It is imparted under supervision and guidance of trained and experienced person(s) in social work. Therefore, it is seen as a two-way process. The student is helped through social work supervision, so that he can work in a complex, intricate and composite social environment. In simple words it can be said that theory without practice is empty and practice without theory is meaningless.

Definitions of Fieldwork

The term "fieldwork" may be described as gaining experience by utilising knowledge and developing the skills to deal with the problems of human beings. *The Dictionary of Sociology* defines fieldwork as "social survey or process of collecting primary data from a population distributed geographically." This is true in a strictly sociological sense, but the meaning of fieldwork in social work is different. A few definitions of fieldwork training in social work education as defined by professional scholars are given under:

(i) Fieldwork in social work education means any kind of practical experience in a social organisation or agency, if this experience has been deliberately arranged, for the education of the students who are undertaking the courses partly or wholly designed for those who intend to become social workers.

(ii) Fieldwork in social work education is a guided interactive process between a student and a social life situation. In this, social work as a profession has an abiding and deep concern that needs to be addressed, remedied, improved or changed for a fuller (a richer) development of human environmental potentials.

(iii) Fieldwork in social work is carried out in and through social welfare agencies and communities, where the student learns skills, tests out knowledge according to an educational plan. The whole programme is, student- and-field specific. Fieldwork training is a supervised practice of student social worker under the guidance of a trained social work educator or field personnel. It has been defined as educationally sponsored attachment of social work students to an institution, agency, or a section of community in which they are helped to extend their knowledge, understand and experience the impact of human needs. Such an experience is deliberately arranged on a whole or part time basis.

Objectives of Fieldwork

Social work is a professional education aimed at helping students to acquire a deep knowledge of theory and techniques, of achieving social work objectives and goals. Students are expected to learn every practical aspect in a three-year graduation course or two years post-graduate training, to acquire an understanding of the principles, concepts, policies and processes that constitute the profession of social work. Through fieldwork programme, students are helped to become competent professional social workers. The general objective of fieldwork training to students is to make them learn and practise those professional social work skills in the field, which are taught in the classrooms. The students try to interpret and diagnose the situation, understand and help people to adjust to the situations in the field. Thus, fieldwork aims at equipping the students to deal with complex problems and personalities. The direct interaction with people helps them to add to their knowledge of people, increase understanding of people's problems and bring emotional power of judgement and stability in action. This is the educational need of the students of social work. The Social Review Committee (1978) on Social Work Education in India has evolved specific objectives of fieldwork training in social work education. The major objectives of fieldwork are as under:

- To develop professional skills through practical learning, apply acquired knowledge for the study of relevant facts, analysis of the problem and selection of appropriate means of solutions towards the problems.
- To develop the skills for solving the problems in work at the micro level (individual), family, groups and communities and the change at macro level in social institutions and processes (types of skills vary with the level of training).
- To provide concurrent opportunity for the integration of classroom learning, in field practice and vice versa (feed-back mechanism for both field and class).
- To develop the skills required for professional practice at a particular level of training.
- To objectively develop professional attitudes involving impartiality and non-judgemental attitudes.
- To develop professional values and commitments, such as respect for human dignity and worth, to the right of participation and self-determination compatible with a better society.
- To develop an awareness of self and one's professional ideas.

The Delhi School of Social Work, which is affiliated to the University of Delhi, had organised a faculty development programme on "Fieldwork in Social Work Education" from March

16 to 19, 1981, and framed specific objectives of fieldwork training as under:

- To offer purposeful learning experience to students through interaction with life situations under supervisory guidance for professional growth in terms of knowledge, skills and attitudes.
- To foster attitudes in the students towards professional growth in terms of knowledge, skills and attitudes.
- To develop in students the required skills in helping the needy through organisational work, use of social work methods, i.e., listening, participation, observation, interaction, communication and so on.
- To enable students to develop and deepen their capacity to relate theory to practice and also to relate experience to theory.

The objectives of fieldwork training in social work education ultimately depend upon the educational and service objectives of social work which are related to the knowledge, skills, attitudes, perspective and action within a dynamic theoretical framework. Thus, the objectives of fieldwork training in social work education can be consolidated to make them easy to study, and understand them clearly so as to have practical experiences accordingly, because these objectives provide learning in the following areas:

- Participation in the process of helping and change.
- Development of positive attitudes, towards self and others.
- Acquisition and development of skills in collaborative teamwork, planning and organisation.
- Experience of shouldering responsibility to deal with critical situations.
- Experience of confrontation with oneself as a means of self-growth and its use in action.

Fieldwork Curriculum

Agency supervisors and trainee students are always in need of practical curriculum for fieldwork training. But, the schools of social work in the country have no specific fieldwork training programme. The trainees go to the agencies without any preparation. This is mainly because of the negligence on the part of the theoreticians. Moreover, the contents of fieldwork training vary at different levels in different fields. Therefore, the question always raised is whether the contents of fieldwork training should be kept common to all the fields and methods of social work. Considering the practical and genuine difficulties, the contents of fieldwork training should vary from agency to agency and also from one specialisation to another. Thus, the content of fieldwork requires certain phases, which are mostly common to both–the fields and methods–of social work.

To impart fieldwork training methodically and scientifically the content of fieldwork training ultimately must comprise of a special programme for different agencies. For example, the content in a hospital setting or health setting should be different from that in a community setting. Similarly, the content of fieldwork training for casework should be different from that for group work or community organisation. As regards specialisation, the content of fieldwork training for labour welfare and family welfare programmes should be different. Thus, the nature of training depends upon the field and method of training. The Delhi School of Social Work had initiated procedures to outline the phases and the content of fieldwork training in general along with the training programme in different fields as under:

(i) Orientation training in social welfare agencies
(ii) Concurrent training in social welfare agencies
(iii) Exploration and assessment
(iv) Evaluation of work or training

Orientation Training in Social Welfare Agency

(1) Introduction of Fields

The introduction phase is expected to familiarise the students with the fields of social work, fieldwork curriculum, the areas and the agencies.

(2) Agency Visits

This includes visits of social settings, i.e., institutions and communities, and recording and report writing on field visits. In the (institutional) field visits the student should be guided in the following areas:

(i) historical background of the region and growth of the institutions;

(ii) objectives and goals of the institutions;
(iii) organisation and structure of the institutions;
(iv) financial position and sources of income or finance and the methods of fund raising, planning and execution;
(v) intake policy of the organisation, procedure and services rendered;
(vi) programmes of the agencies and their relationship with objectives and goals of the institution; and
(vii) facilities provided to the employees, beneficiaries and the problems faced by the institutions.

(3) Community Visits

In case of the visits to the community the students should be provided guidelines as follows:
(i) history of the community (perspective and retrospective);
(ii) composition of the community (religion, caste, language, occupation, sex and the like);
(iii) various facilities available to the people from the government, social institutions and voluntary organisations;
(iv) existing and functioning organisations in the community (general and community development projects, ideal projects, etc.); and
(v) problems faced by the community in general, and the society in particular.

Concurrent Fieldwork Training

In this second phase of fieldwork training students should be placed in the agencies according to their field of interest and should be provided guidelines as under:

(1) Introduction

(i) introduction to the fieldwork requirements and its procedure;
(ii) introduction to fieldwork practice in the agency/community; and
(iii) introduction to the client system.

(2) Work Assignment

The second aspect of content of placement related to work assignment is as under:

(i) definite work assignment,
(ii) definite target group, and
(iii) work assignment, which may evolve out of exploration by the students themselves.

(3) Exploration and Assessment

In the third phase exploration, assessment, action, etc., should be covered. The content under this phase is formulated as under:

(i) need identification and resource mobilisation;
(ii) programme development;
(iii) assumption, social work, roles and professional involvement;
(iv) individual conferences;
(v) group conferences;
(vi) fieldwork seminars;
(vii) recording; and
(viii) on-going assessment and prospective guidance.

(4) Evaluation of Students' Performance

In the fourth phase of fieldwork training evaluation of students performance should be done at four different levels based on the following contents:

(i) summary records and other records;
(ii) personal qualities and professional skills; and
(iii) capability of relating theory to practice:
    - student self-evaluation,
    - agency's evaluation,
    - fieldwork supervisor's evaluation, and
    - school or external examiner's evaluation.

Field Practicum of Minnesota University

The University Fieldwork Coordinator of the Minnesota University, USA, has prepared a curriculum guide of fieldwork programmes, for the purposes of setting a pattern for any agency participating in field instruction programme. According to this curriculum, the content is divided into three learning areas:

- Factual content,
- Problem-solving/inventing content, and
- Self-understanding/awareness content.

Components of Fieldwork

There are four components of fieldwork training in social work education:

(i) the social welfare agency,
(ii) the trainee student,
(iii) the faculty supervisor, and
(iv) the agency supervisor.

The agency and faculty supervisors aim at imparting training to students who are learners. The students operate between the client or group, the agency and the supervisors. Fieldwork agencies provide an opportunity to the students to exercise theory, principles and philosophy of social work taught in schools. These social agencies play a vital role in fieldwork training due to which they are called training workshops of the schools of social work. Yet, due attention is not given to these agencies, either by the schools or by the management of these agencies, with a view to creating a proper infrastructure.

Students are placed in the agencies for fieldwork training throughout the academic year, and it is expected that they become a part of the agencies. In fact, for all practical purposes, students need to be accepted as members of the social agency.

In the process of fieldwork, students undergo training under the guidance of the trained persons, and therefore, they are required to maintain professional relations with the agencies and the trainers. However, this does not mean that they have nothing to do with those others concerned, who furnish information for the purpose of practical learning. Every person concerned with the training is equally important. The students should maintain professional relations with each one of them. Moreover, placement of the students are with the agency and not with the supervisors. Naturally, they learn from all the concerned employees of the respective agencies. The schools maintain a cordial relationship through the students with the concerned fieldwork agencies. These three components of fieldwork training are in no way different, they are actually interrelated to one another.

Problems in Fieldwork

The schools of social work in India face many problems. These problems begin with the placement of the students and end with the evaluation of their performance. The problems can again be classified into three specific groups, viz., School Specific, Student Specific and Agency Specific. The major problems of the schools of social work in India in general and their impact on training are as under:

School-Specific

(i) Finding suitable agencies and developing them as workshops for the students of social work education thereby restricting the scope of fieldwork training.

(ii) Lack of practical-oriented faculty, due to which the schools are not in a position to impart training in social work education in a professional and practical sense.

(iii) Lack of suitable content of fieldwork training due to which the training cannot be imparted as per the expectations of professional social work.

(iv) Lack of a fieldwork manual, due to which students are often confused as to what kind of work is to be carried out in the agencies during the training period throughout the academic year.

(v) Dearth of literature on fieldwork, due to which students are unable to understand the concepts clearly from a practical point of view.

(vi) Lack of the required work culture in the schools due to which fieldwork is not practised rigorously.

(vii) Lack of healthy competition in the field due to which the schools are not able to maintain a standard of fieldwork training in social work education.

Agency-Specific

(i) Lack of the required work culture in the agencies due to which fieldwork is not practised rigorously.

(ii) Lack of trained social work manpower in most of the agencies, thus affecting the nature of training in social work education.

(iii) Semi-trained persons either as the head or as a supervisor due to which the quality of the fieldwork training gets affected.

Student-Specific

(i) Non-availability of meritorious students opting for social work as a profession, due to which the products coming out of the field of social work are poor and weak.

(ii) Examination-orientation of the students due to which professional approach is not developed in the field.

These are the general problems identified. These and a host of other smaller ones together have today paralysed fieldwork training in social work education. Unless all these are addressed systematically, there lies little hope for the future.

Nature and Structure of Fieldwork

There seems to be no uniformity in the fieldwork systems being practised in the schools of social work in India today. The number of days of fieldwork in a week, seems to vary from school to school. There are some schools which have introduced fieldwork for two days in a week whereas others have stipulated three days and the students are asked to work for 15 to 20 hours in a week. As far as the number of visits to the agencies for concurrent fieldwork are concerned, the schools expect minimum 45 visits for casework, 45 visits for group work or 45 visits for community organisations in an academic year. The students are asked to meet the concerned faculty supervisors in the respective schools to seek guidance before they proceed to the agencies on every fieldwork day. To enable students to learn practicals methodically, they are taught the relevant part of theory in brief prior to their fieldwork assignments, to ensure conceptual clarity. The necessary points of study are given to them and the students are supposed to record these points in their diaries every week on fieldwork days. After seeking guidance from the faculty/supervisors, the students proceed to their agencies for practical work. Here again, the agency supervisors guide them in the procedure, methods and practices to be followed for learning in practical situations. It is always expected that the students should bridge the gap between theory and practice and learn practicals quickly to develop their professional skills, knowledge, attitudes, etc. The faculty supervisors also pay visits to the agencies and help students to learn methodically and use social work techniques and skills.

It is very important that a consistency be brought into the entire system of fieldwork training. With this in mind the author suggests the following:

- Fieldwork should be a uniform three days of eight hours each, every week.
- In moffussil areas the approach should be need-based and integrated. In other word, direct methods, viz., casework, group work, community organisation and indirect methods, viz., social welfare administration, social work research and social action should be integrated.

Fieldwork Supervision

The primary responsibility of the fieldwork supervisor is to teach and develop fieldwork curriculum, integration of theory and field practice, creation of an atmosphere or environment, in which a student can learn. Besides this, it is the duty of the supervisor to teach students the meaning of professional relationship, to deepen their insight into their own behaviours and that of others, to teach the techniques of interviewing, recording, home visits and such other skills, as are necessary for successful discharge of the students' professional responsibilities. In other words, it can be said that the supervisor teaches particularly about concepts, skills and attitudes and performs three major roles of teaching, administering and helping. But, the function of teaching occupies a significant role in the process of fieldwork training. The Delhi School of Social Work has delineated the roles of the supervisor into different phases as follows:

Orientation Training Phase

The faculty supervisor has to narrate and explain the fieldwork programme of the school to the students and the process of social work supervision, roles and functions of the supervisor, the general idea about the fields of social work and general expectation of the students.

Induction Training Phase

In the induction phase, the faculty supervisor has to introduce the agency or fields to the students. He has to explain the role of students in the client system and nature of client systems. He also has to guide the students at different levels in establishing professional relationship with the agency supervisor, relating to the agency supervisor's methods in achieving the objectives and goals of the agency. He also has to guide the students in report preparation, etc.

Practical Implementation Phase

In implementation phase the faculty supervisor should help students to identify the needs, arrange resources to evolve work assignments, clarify doubts, share their experiences, foster growth and awareness in students. Similarly, they should assist the school in administration, development of relationship between the agency and the school, etc.

Fieldwork Evaluation Phase

In the evaluation phase the faculty supervisor should help the school and students to formulate a pattern of evaluation on the basis of his experience and help them devise evaluation procedures and processes.

Methods of Fieldwork Supervision

The methods of fieldwork supervision are based on and related to its functions, which are spread throughout the procedure of supervision, right from the orientation programme till the end of training. Attempts are made by the supervisors to help students in attaining the skills. The steps and methods are important because they are certainly helpful in attaining the educational goals of fieldwork training in social work. The following methods are practised in the schools:

- Individual conference of faculty and students,
- Group conference of faculty and students,
- Fieldwork seminars of the students, and
- On-the-spot instructions of the faculty supervisors.

Individual Conference of Faculty and Students

To impart fieldwork training methodically the supervisors conduct individual conferences with the students on every fieldwork day either in the schools or in the agencies. Individual conference is nothing but purposeful interaction between the students and the supervisors in terms of fieldwork training in social work education. The objectives of such conferences are as under:

(i) To give individual attention to the students, so as to assess the student's ability to understand fieldwork process, for the purpose of guiding them in practicals;
(ii) To assist students in identifying their weakness during practicals;
(iii) To study the procedures and processes followed and to make use of the principles, philosophy and techniques in practice, and to inculcate in the students a scientific approach; and
(iv) To foster, develop and nurture a professional relationship between the students and faculty supervisors, and also to generate confidence in the students.

Group Conferences of Faculty and Students

Group conferences are also conducted during the fieldwork. The conference is conducted either in the schools or in the agencies to educate the students in the group process. The objectives of group conferences are as under:

(i) To exchange ideas of each group, to enhance each group's practical knowledge gained through their fieldwork and help them to learn from each other;
(ii) To develop mutual support and increase intergroup co-operation in the field; and
(iii) To assist the students in boosting their confidence through group interaction.

Fieldwork Seminars of the Students

The fieldwork seminars are also conducted by the faculty supervisors to enable the students to learn how to present the work done by them in the fieldwork agency, methods used for doing it systematically, the social work skills used and developed. This also develops their art of presentation, self-confidence and helps them overcome stage fear.

Spot Instructions by the Faculty Supervisor

The faculty supervisors visit the agencies and help the students learn in practical situations by giving them on-the-spot instructions in connection with various aspects of the study, and enable them to carry out their work systematically and scientifically.

Recording: Diaries and Journals

The concurrent fieldwork continues throughout the academic year, which enables students to learn a great deal on every fieldwork day. However, it is very difficult to remember each and every aspect at the end of the fieldwork. So it is necessary to maintain a record of the practical work for remembrance, guidance and evaluation of their performance, in the form of diaries and journals separately for casework and group work. Though students maintain diaries and journals accordingly, most of them are not aware of the basic purpose of maintaining them. The purpose of maintaining diaries are discussed below:

Purpose of a Casework Diary

(i) The process of casework is lengthy and it is difficult for the student caseworker to retain all the information collected from the clients, their relatives, friends, neighbours and the concerned persons during the process of casework and the steps taken by them in dealing with the case. The information recorded in the diaries in brief enables the caseworkers to refer to this whenever required, when dealing with clients.

(ii) The students can take guidance from the concerned faculty supervisors, to learn the casework process, the brief recording enables the supervisors to refer to or read the recorded information in the diaries and guide the students for further practice. This continues till all the cases are solved.

(iii) The brief recording in the diaries also helps the students to write cases in detail in their journals which creates a literature on social casework for the development of casework theory.

Purpose of a Group Work Diary

(i) To record group work programmes and reactions of the group members observed during the process of group work in brief.

This enables the group work student to refer to it for the purpose of processing the personality development of the group members whenever needed.

(ii) The brief recording in diaries is necessary for concerned faculty supervisors for the purpose of future guidance and this continues till the end of the course.

(iii) The brief recording in diaries also assists the students to write their journals in detail whenever needed.

Procedure for Submission of Diary

Students are instructed to maintain diaries, for recording in brief, the practical work done by them in their respective agencies, to get the signatures of the agency supervisor on every fieldwork day, and to submit them to the concerned faculty supervisors on every fieldwork day. This recording enables the faculty supervisors to know the learning process, ability, speed and need of the students and guide them in further processes. This procedure seems to be strictly practised in almost every school.

Procedure for Submission of Journals

Students are asked to write their journals in detail on the basis of the recordings in the diaries and to submit them to the concerned faculty supervisors once every week, fortnight or month for checking and evaluating their work and actual performance. The policy of the schools as regards the submission of the journals differs in different schools.

Evaluation of Fieldwork Performance

Generally, the evaluation of the performance of the students is done by the concerned supervisors every month/quarter/half year to enable them to understand the abilities and progress of the students. This is normally done in two ways: (i) self-evaluation, and (ii) experts' evaluation. Two-way evaluations help the students to clear their confusions. They also enable the teachers to bring to the notice of the students their inadequacies so that the students can overcome these and grow into perfect professionals.

Think and Do

"Social work is a professional and practising course like medical or engineering is, that provides an opportunity to set up an independent voluntary organisation providing self-employment and rendering social service."

Chapter 2

Fieldwork Supervision

"Fieldwork supervision teaches the students to integrate theory and practice in the field. It creates an environment in which professional skills for social work practice can be learnt."

The word `supervision' consists of two different words super and vision. `Super' means over and above, and `vision' means the art of seeing objects, or perceiving a mental image, or looking over. The traditional and literary meaning of the term supervision is interpreted differently. The traditional meaning of the term is inspection. In inspection, the supervisor gives instructions, checks to see weather the instructions have been carried out in their true sense and uses power to control the people who work under him. The literal meaning is overseeing.

The characteristic of supervision is to see that the work assigned is accomplished as directed and expected. If it is not accomplished then the supervisors are held responsible and answerable. The main functions of supervision are administration and teaching. The administrative function is nothing but watching over the work assigned to people, regulating it and controlling the quality of work in terms of administrative policies and procedure of the organisation. The teaching function of supervision is to guide recipients with a view to improving their practical knowledge, professional skills and work techniques is the respective fields.

Various scholars have defined the term supervision. A few have been quoted here.

> Supervision is the achievement of desired results through intelligent utilisation of human talents and facilitating resources in a manner that provides the greatest challenge and interest to the human talents. –George R. Terry

> Supervision is a traditional method of transmitting knowledge of social work skills in practice from the trained to the untrained, from the experienced to the inexperienced student and worker.
>
> –*Encyclopedia of Social Work*, 1965

> Supervision is an administrative function, a process for getting the work done and maintaining organisational control and accountability.
>
> –*Encyclopedia of Social Work*, 1971-77

> Social work supervision is an administrative process with an educational purpose.
>
> –Towle

Fieldwork Supervision

With specific relation to social work education, both the traditional and literal concepts of supervision have no place. In social work, `supervision' is regarded as a helping process, in which the supervisor helps the students in doing their assigned work and helps them increase their abilities and capacities to serve the poor, needy, helpless and sufferers. The term `supervision' in social work education was defined by trained social workers during a workshop that was held on "Fieldwork Training in Social Work Education", organised by the University of Delhi. A few have been quoted here:

> Supervision is an educational, administrative and helping process which is concerned with enabling, teaching and guiding a supervisee to develop professional skills, knowledge and attitudes based on the objectives of an educational programme and the needs of the supervisor.

> Supervisory process is both creative and dynamic and it calls for investment by the supervisor in terms of knowledge, attitudes, skills and perspective in guiding a student to meet the demands of learning as well as that of the field.

The concept of fieldwork supervision in social work education is dual:

(i) supervision by the faculty members, and
(ii) supervision by the practitioners or agency supervisors.

The faculty members guide the students in understanding the concepts and techniques of social work, principles and philosophies of social work, procedures and methods of practising social work theories and the utility value for social work practice. They help the students in preparing themselves to be theoretically sound and make them conceptually clear to anchor theories in practice for effective professional services.

The practitioners or the agency supervisors guide the students in acquiring professional skills, knowledge, procedure and methods of social work and the use of techniques in the actual field for rendering welfare services and for solving the problems of the needy, helpless, poor and sufferers.

To acquire professional skills the following two components are considered very important: (i) the faculty supervisors, and (ii) the practitioners or agency supervisors. The former assist in theory and practice and the latter in practical guidance, assignment of relevant practical work and overseeing the work from the social work perspective.

In other words, the term `supervision' in social work education is "an educational process in which a person, a supervisor, a more knowledgeable and professionally competent individual imparts designed concepts, skills and attitudes to students, through various educational tools like supervisory interactions, supervisory relationships, professional skills and techniques and the supervisory individual and group conferences". The functions of supervision in social work education are to facilitate, accelerate, smoothen and consolidate the students' learning in practical situations. It can be said that social work supervision is meant for an educational partnership of two individuals, viz., the faculty supervisors or the practitioner supervisors and the students. The supervisors are more experienced, knowledgeable, mature and have social perspective and human understanding while the students are those who have set out to acquire knowledge of theory and practice, professional skills, techniques and the methods required for a professional social worker.

The supervisory process in social work aims at the development of field practicum, integration of theory and practice and creation of an environment through which the students should be able to learn practical aspects of social work theories and philosophies. It rests upon democratic values and ideals, which are not the denial of responsibilities. Hence, social work supervision has incorporated the following aspects into it:

(i) A conscious common purpose to help the students to achieve the desired goal of becoming professionally trained social workers.
(ii) A common interest in the welfare of people and the value of social services.
(iii) A professional contact with knowledgeable persons, with tested skills and objectives, with whom students can identify.
(iv) A mutual understanding and agreement as to the respective roles and responsibilities of the students and both categories of supervisors, viz., faculty supervisors and practitioner supervisors.
(v) A clarification of the conditions and procedures as to what is expected to be accomplished, when and why.
(vi) An opportunity for reciprocal communication, which makes identification with both the supervisors possible, as a source of learning for the students.
(vii) Both faculty supervisors and practitioner supervisors should possess a sense of humour, affection for their fellowmen, and an ability to help the students understand what is happening in the practical field/reality.

Objectives of Fieldwork Supervision

The general and specific objectives of fieldwork supervision in social work education are as follows:

(i) To provide an opportunity to the students to learn social work techniques in practical situations in different fields and to meet the needs of professional education.
(ii) To organise and accelerate the process of learning practical aspects of social work theories and philosophies in the different fields of social work.
(iii) To facilitate achievement of learning goals especially practical use of principles and philosophies, skill and techniques, in social work practice.
(iv) To enable the students to enhance their practical knowledge and to develop their art of dealing with humans in various situations.
(v) To help the students acquire professional skills and to develop their social attitudes.

(vi) To help the students to assess their strengths and weaknesses in proper perspective.
(vii) To assist the students in developing their social perspectives and social outlook for effective social work practice.
(viii) To enable the students enhance their interest in social work profession.
(ix) To help the students acquire sound practical knowledge, and help them to build a career in the field of social work.

The specific objective of fieldwork supervision is to regulate the fieldwork programmes and to bring out the consistency in the fieldwork process as a whole, through various supervisory functions.

Functions of the Faculty Supervisors

The prime responsibility of the faculty supervisors is to teach the students theory and to orient them to practice, in their respective fields. To carry out these prime responsibilities they have to take interest in framing the field practicum on the basis of the needs of the profession, the field agencies and the students, and revise it from time to time.

With the help of the developed field practical and theoretical curriculum the faculty supervisors have to guide and assist the students, to integrate theory with practicals and to create an environment for them to learn in practical situations.

Faculty supervisors have to teach the students fieldwork i.e., the meaning of professional relationship, to develop an insight into their own and others' behaviours, to help them grasp the techniques of interviewing, recording, conducting home visits and such other skills, as are necessary for successful discharge of their professional responsibilities. In other words, the faculty supervisors have to teach three main things: (i) concepts of social work in fieldwork, (ii) social work techniques and professional skills, and (iii) social attitudes and perspectives. They find meaning in these three functions as field administration, fieldwork teaching and professional help. However, of all these functions, the teaching function occupies a very significant place in the process of fieldwork training in social work education.

Trained professional social workers have narrated the roles of the faculty supervisors during the various phases in the workshop

"Fieldwork Training in Social Work Education", organised by the Delhi School of Social Work Education as follows:

Orientation Phase

The faculty supervisors have to narrate the fieldwork programmes of their schools to the students and must explain the process of supervision and their roles and functions.

A general idea should be given to the students regarding the fields of social work and explain them their expectations from the students about professional training in social work.

Induction Phase

The faculty supervisors have to introduce their students to the social welfare agencies or communities where they will be placed for concurrent fieldwork. It is also expected that the client system is narrated to the students and the roles of the students in the client system are explained. Students should be re-conditioned at different levels and should be told about the supervisor-supervisee relationship. They must also help the students in establishing this relationship so as to carry out the functions of guidance on fieldwork and report writing and ultimately achieve the goals of fieldwork training.

Implementation Phase

The faculty supervisors have to help the students identify the needs and resources, and to evolve work assignments. Similarly, they have to help the students to learn in practical situations. The faculty supervisors have to clear doubts in terms of solving the problems of the client/needy and sufferers. The supervisee should be helped to share his/her experiences so as to be able to analyse feelings. The supervisor should then extend support to the students in achieving faster growth and awareness. Besides these, the faculty supervisors are expected to conduct on-the-spot supervision and administration, and develop relations between the agency and schools throughout the implementation phase.

Evaluation Phase

The faculty supervisors have to formulate a pattern of evaluation and help in the evaluation. They must assist the schools in maintaining records of fieldwork for inspection by the university or external examiners.

Functions of the Agency Supervisors

The professional responsibility of agency supervisors is to guide the students on office procedures and methods so that they understand the functions of the agencies. Instructions have to be given on methods and techniques of social work, in dealing with individual groups and communities, professional interactions, use of principles and philosophies of social work in the field, etc. Students must also be instructed on how to create an atmosphere of work and to render professional services to solve the problems of the clients.

The agency supervisors have to teach the students on how to maintain professional relations with individual clients, groups, communities, members and employees of the agencies. They also have to teach them the expected, mature and polished behaviour in dealing with everyone concerned. Besides this, their responsibility is also to shape the students' views and to build a personality suitable for a professional social worker. The necessary guidelines are to be given and their social outlooks and perspectives are to be enhanced. In other words, it can be said that the agency supervisors have to teach three main aspects:

(a) Principles and philosophy of social work and use of these in practice for providing solutions to problems of individuals, groups and communities. These are to be accomplished with the help of all three direct social work methods namely casework, group work and community organisation, and the three indirect methods, namely, social welfare administration, social work research and social action.

(b) Professional skills of handling human beings in good and bad situations, to solve their problems, to enhance their confidence and to make them capable enough to help themselves in life.

(c) Official correspondence especially in relation to preparation of case sheets, reports, proposals, rehabilitative reports, handling of accounts and administrative paper work related to conducting meetings, agency proceedings, decisions, etc., and general letters to make the students administrative oriented and capable enough to handle an office on their own in future.

All three functions of the agency supervisors occupy a very significant place in the process of imparting practical training in social work education because each in themselves will enable the students to become able professional social work practitioners.

Methods of Faculty Supervision

Social work supervision starts right from the orientation period to the end of concurrent fieldwork training. Throughout this process the faculty supervisor makes an attempt to help the students acquire professional knowledge and skills, using different techniques and methods. These methods are very important because they help in achieving the targets or goals of social work supervision. These methods are based on the functions of supervision which are spread throughout the supervisory procedure as follows:

(i) Individual conference,
(ii) Group conference,
(iii) Spot instructions, and
(iv) Fieldwork seminars.

However, to support the supervisory programmes and relationships certain principles related to supervisory methods are essential to be observed. They are as follows:

(i) Faculty supervisors should be available and be frank to the valid needs of the situations, i.e., all kinds of learning needs.
(ii) The students should be encouraged by faculty supervisors to be self-reliant in areas in which they have necessary knowledge and competence to function independently.
(iii) While strengths of the students should be pointed out, the faculty supervisors should not shirk their responsibility of helping students in overcoming problems due to inadequacies in field performance.
(iv) The faculty supervisors should overlook unrealistic demands of the students and meet only the realistic ones.
(v) The students should be made to focus professionally on services to their clients on the basis of clients' needs.
(vi) The first supervisory conference should be planned to set the tone for the supervisor and the student, with proper allocation

of responsibilities between them.

(vii) Regular time for tutorials should be arranged to avoid interruptions and the students should be encouraged to utilise this time for seeking clarifications including urgent issues. However, it must be made very clear to them that they can seek additional help whenever needed.

(viii) The importance of orientation and, well thought out and planned induction eases out anxiety and helps the students to begin their functions on a more confident note.

(ix) The students should be made to actively participate in the learning functions in terms of, what they think, what they need to know, etc., in order to get started and to keep up their practice of formulation. They should be helped to carry out their responsibilities towards the services to the clients.

(x) The students should be prompt in recording, and utilising such recordings as a basic teaching and learning tool in supervision discussions.

(xi) The students should be assigned fieldwork immediately and should start working on the assigned project/work.

(xii) The faculty supervisors should focus the identification of feelings of the students towards learning and they should see that the students do not lose track of their responsibilities.

(xiii) Students should be provided with an opportunity to develop their own professional styles and they should be allowed to find their own ways of applying the principles of social work.

(xiv) Students should be adequately encouraged to learn every aspect sincerely. The faculty supervisors should make the students understand that the supervisory process is to help them meet the difficult demands of any situation relating to the client without causing any damage.

Methods of Agency Supervision

Agency supervision starts with the placement of students in their respective agencies for concurrent fieldwork. The process of agency supervision begins with the introduction of the students to the agency supervisors, the concerned employees of the agencies, the social structure and systems of the agencies, their programmes, beneficiaries, work methods and procedures, and social work techniques used in the agencies.

The agency supervisors use different methods of supervision to help the students acquire necessary professional skills, knowledge of different fields and various social work techniques. These methods help the students achieve professional training goals. They are spread throughout the supervision procedure.

(i) Professional interaction with faculty supervisors for processing fieldwork.
(ii) Professional orientation of the fields and social welfare agencies.
(iii) Guidance to the students for observation in the fields or agencies.
(iv) Guidance to the student for professional interactions with clients or needy persons.
(v) Guidance to the students for collection of field information by using survey method.
(vi) Guidance to the students for collection of relevant papers.
(vii) Professional instructions to the students both oral and written, to work with individuals, groups and communities.
(viii) Professional interaction with the students and professional observation of the actual work
(ix) Help the students to observe and participate in work processes of the agency.
(x) Help the students to observe and organise functions.
(xi) Help the students to observe and prepare records for the purpose.
(xii) Help the students establish contact with concerned people to help them in finding solutions to the problems.

Problems in Fieldwork Supervision

Social work supervision in the field, in terms of training has many problems. Both faculty supervisors as well as agency supervisors face various problems relating to the students and their training in social work and training systems. The three components of fieldwork training, viz., the students, the supervisors and the agencies are significant factors of practical training in the fields/agencies. And each throws up problems of its own. These have been discussed below:

Problems Relating to the Students

(i) In general, it is seen that meritorious students of different disciplines do not come to the schools of social work to build a career in professional social work, due to which those who do get admitted seem to be lacking in professional interest which is a major hurdle in effective social work supervision.

(ii) The lack of taking initiatives on the part of the student in the field of social work is one of the basic problems of supervision. The learning is affected, as also the services rendered to the agency.

(iii) The placement of the students in the agencies without considering their interest is one of the causes of students' ineffectiveness in the agencies and it becomes difficult for the supervisors to generate interest in such students.

(iv) The lack of social attitudes and social perspectives of the students is also one of the problems worth consideration in supervision. Till these are instilled and developed the students are not able to grasp practical aspects easily. Their concentration is often disturbed and these are responsible for poor learning.

(v) The lethargic attitude of degree-oriented students is also one of the problems of supervision. Such students do not work sincerely and honestly, either in the agencies or on the field. To make such students learn and work is a real headache for the supervisors.

(vi) The influence of the western life style on the attitudes of the students is another problem in supervision. It has become difficult for supervisors to produce trained professional social workers who do not have any bad habits. This has become one of the hurdles in bringing pride to the profession of social work.

Problems Pertaining to the Faculty Supervisors

(i) Untrained supervisors, appointed in some of the schools of social work, find it difficult to guide students on social work techniques, social work principles and philosophies, for acquiring professional skills.

(ii) Trained faculty members also face difficulties in guiding students in solving their field problems due to lack of practical experience. Their genuine difficulties become a problem for the schools and the students in terms of qualitative professional supervision.

(iii) The allotment of a number of agencies to the faculty supervisors is yet another problem. In addition to the time consumed in visiting each of them, personal money is spent in paying visits to these agencies because schools do not reimburse the same. Due to this, faculty members avoid visiting all the allotted agencies.

(iv) The lack of infrastructure and facilities in the schools reduces faculty supervisors' interest in developing and implementing the field practicum. As a result, they become lethargic after a few years. Ultimately this becomes a problem of the faculty members, students and also the schools.

(v) Faculty supervisors do not get cooperation and appreciation from academic leaders in most of the schools despite putting in sincere and valuable effort, time, labour, energy, intellectual contribution and exemplary work. The non-cooperative attitude and lack of appreciation from the leaders also contributes towards the non-effective supervision by the faculty supervisors.

(vi) The lack of understanding on the part of the academic leaders and security of services is also one of the important problems of the faculty supervisors which hinders sincere working in the field with the students.

Problems Pertaining to the Agency Supervisors

(i) One of the problems of the agency supervisors is in terms of the amount of time to be given to the students and the faculty supervisors for fieldwork training because they have to shoulder this training in addition to the responsibilities of the agencies.

(ii) The agency supervisor faces problems in the agencies in terms of imparting training to the students, i.e., expectations of the schools are not in line with what the agencies can offer to the students.

(iii) The agency supervisors are usually not aware of the type of assignment the students propose to carry out with the clients or groups during the fieldwork placement.

(iv) The agency supervisors have to function as supervisors of the students, without any additional remuneration being received and without any appreciation of their work, from either the concerned schools and agencies or communities and government.

(v) There is a problem in providing continuity in learning due to change of placement of the students or completion of the academic term or assigned work. This makes the agency supervisors helpless in supervising the students continuously and making them adequately trained within the allotted time.

(vi) Students as learners do not morally associate themselves with the fieldwork agencies, due to which it becomes difficult for agency supervisors to keep the former closely related to the agency services.

(vii) The students are in the agencies on specified days only for a few hours in a week due to which proper guidance and training cannot be given within the framework of social work education.

(viii) The agency supervisors, if untrained, face problems in guiding and giving instructions to the students as is expected in social work education.

Problems Pertaining to the Agencies

(i) Well established agencies having the goodwill of society and those which share the responsibilities of communities, in general, do not allow students for fieldwork training in their agencies. Even if they do allow, they do not give enough time to the students.

(ii) Many social welfare agencies do not have well set programmes, qualified and experienced staff, good standards of services, etc., which otherwise provide a rich learning experience to the students in the agencies.

(iii) Many social welfare agency workers feel that students are sometimes quite critical about the workers' services towards the community, and thus create problems due to which the real practices are not demonstrated to the students. Complete or relevant information in such cases, is not divulged to the students. This hesitation or fear is one of the major problems of the agencies.

(iv) Since students are fresh and the agencies cannot utilise their services, they feel that imparting training to the students is but a time-consuming and fruitless job to be done as a ritual. Besides, they are quite unaware of how to help the faculty supervisors become closely related to the agency work.

(v) Most agencies cannot afford to have audio-visual equipment for imparting training due to which effective training cannot be given. They still follow the old and traditional methods, like explanations, discussions, lectures, etc.

(vi) Records of social work done by the agencies are confidential in nature and cannot be shared with the students while imparting training. But without showing the records fieldwork training cannot be imparted in its real sense. This is a handicap which becomes a problem to the supervisor to effectively perform the role of a trainer.

Problems Pertaining to the Schools

(i) The intake policy of the concerned universities and the schools is one of the major problems in terms of fieldwork supervision. Many a time, students are more in number, which creates the problem of allotment to the faculty supervisors. Moreover, schools cannot bring down the strength of the students nor can the staff strength be increased. The increased social work supervision is therefore allotted to the existing faculty supervisors. This affects the sincerity and quality of the faculty supervisors.

(ii) Agencies are normally geographically spread out in different areas and the distance between them is a problem in terms of making regular visits. The management of neither the schools nor the UGC nor the state or central governments, provide any vehicle facilities to the schools for fieldwork visits. The schools then insist that faculties use their own vehicles, which acts as a disincentive to the supervisors.

(iii) Universities and state governments do not sanction a separate post for fieldwork in a school to make fieldwork strong, effective and systematic. This shortcoming has crippled the fieldwork system and the quality of training imparted by schools of social work. The faculty themselves have to look into both the theory and the practicals.

(iv) The state government and the universities grant permission to start new institutions in some states without considering the need for it and the number of suitable agencies available in those areas. The placement of additional students in such agencies by every school adds to the constraints in terms of time and energy to be spared by the agencies.

(v) In most cities, agencies operating in different fields are not available for effective and overall training needs of the students. In such cases the schools are forced to place students in adjoining areas, which again create supervision problems

(vi) The concurrent fieldwork days are considered as holidays by some of the faculty supervisors in cases where the academic leader is not a taskmaster, or where insufficient infrastructure and poor facilities are available. In such places the faculty supervisors visit the agencies only when they find time. Mostly it is to check whether the students are present or absent and not with a view to helping the students learn or to solve their problems.

Needs of the Schools for Effective Supervision

To overcome the technical difficulties faced by schools and agencies in solving their supervision problems, the following needs of schools will have to be met by the institutions or persons concerned:

(i) Schools of social work should try and set up different social welfare agencies with the help of associations of trained social workers, funding agencies and the Ministry of Social Welfare. These will not only generate some employment opportunities but will also increase the scope for imparting training to the students of the institute. In addition, the schools can render services to the communities and get social recognition.

(ii) The schools should develop community or rural development projects. Students can be placed in these projects for undergoing training in social work techniques and also learn integrated fieldwork.

(iii) The agency supervisors who render services to the schools for fieldwork training of the students should be given some compensation in terms of money for making their services effective. Schools normally collect fees from the students for fieldwork training. Students are given only journals from this amount. In the present pattern of grant no provision has been made by the government for payment to agency supervisors. It is suggested that some amount from that collection be distributed amongst the agency supervisors for their valuable services.

(iv) The University Grants Commission, New Delhi, has introduced a scheme of providing four wheeler vehicles for fieldwork training. This facility can be made available to those schools of social work which are registered under the UGC Act, 1956. The vehicle can help faculty supervisors to supervise the students more effectively.

(v) Regarding non-payment of conveyance allowance, it is strongly felt that it should be given so that supervision by faculty members becomes more sincere, responsible and effective.

(vi) To impart fieldwork training regularly, schools should delegate authorities and nominate senior faculty as professors in charge of fieldwork training for first year and final year student. These professors should be given freedom to execute the fieldwork programme devised by the schools. This delegation of authority will definitely motivate the supervisors as a result of which their supervisory functions will be more effective.

(vii) The schools should provide certain special facilities to the faculty supervisors like Travel Allowance (TA) and Dearness Allowance (DA) for undergoing practical training in some NGOs or institutions during the mid-term or summer vacations. This will enhance their practical knowledge and in turn they will become effective supervisors.

(viii) Schools should have their own magazines or periodicals and the students should be encouraged to contribute their field experiences. Such collections will be useful to future students and will encourage them and boost their self-confidence regarding writing and presenting the cases handled by them. This practice will definitely assist the supervisors to be active in the field and also to motivate the fieldworkers.

(ix) To provide continuity to specifically handled cases a

recording system should be devised so that a case taken up by students is still dealt with by his successor. Creating a team of two students one each of previous year and final year with steady transition of the incoming and outgoing could be the best solution to providing continuity to cases.

Implementation of Supervisory Instructions

To maintain discipline in the schools, agencies and fields, punctuality and regularity on the part of the students is very important. The principle of self-discipline is the best discipline and the faculty supervisors should practice it. They must try and inculcate this in the personalities of the students.

To help students to be responsible and mature social workers of the future they should be taught etiquette, manners and effective communication skills. The faculty supervisors should observe the behaviour of the students in the agencies and field minutely and try to correct them if they do not follow the supervisory instructions. Observance of these teachings will assist the faculty supervisors to perform effective supervisory functions in terms of qualitative practical training.

The faculty supervisors should make students work in the agencies for eight hours a day. Students who avoid putting in the necessary number of hours and hesitate to render their services should be convinced about its significance as well as about their loss in terms of marks, opportunities of learning in practical situations, etc. In spite of this, if the irregularity continues, they should be dealt with sternly. Any laxity in handling of the situation may jeopardise the discipline in the field, which may affect the supervisory functions and the quality of training.

The faculty supervisors should also be regular and punctual in the field to set an example to the students. An ideal supervisory work culture will be created and developed in the field. Their sincerity and honesty will be useful in building the careers of hundreds of students who will automatically follow the good behavioural pattern.

Students pay fieldwork fees in their respective schools, and the government pays the salary of the faculty supervisors. Both should utilise the opportunity to learn and render services for the agencies and the communities. Both can expect the desired performance from each other and be useful to the society at large. Both should bear in mind that non-utilisation or underutilisation is a loss to the profession.

The fieldwork coordinators and the directors of schools should check the regular functions of the faculty supervisors and pay surprise visits to the agencies to oversee the progress and development. They must also look into the problems faced by students in the field.

For systematic learning by the students, the faculty supervisors should devise learning instructions. They should have individual and group conferences a day before the fieldwork day and give them learning instructions in writing and ask them to follow the same in the agencies/field in consultation with the agency supervisors. The students should be asked to report the day's work in the agencies, on very next day. Such practises will certainly be effective in the learning process. It also assists the schools to develop a rich culture of learning in the field.

Students should be asked to submit their diaries and journals before every fieldwork day for checking. At the same time, directions for the next day's activity can also be given. Such practices will definitely make the students alert, quick, active and prompt in their functions of reporting. The work of checking diaries and journals should be done immediately by the concerned faculty supervisors and directions should be given to the students for further learning process. Such promptness from both of them will create a disciplined order of fieldwork training and supervision.

Think and Do

"Students should take advantage of fieldwork supervision and try to make the best of the situation to learn professional skills and enrich their field knowledge to practice social work in the field on scientific lines for effective solution to the problems of the needy and sufferers in the society."

Chapter 3

Orientation Training

"Orientation training helps students understand the nature and structure of social welfare organisations and scientific social work practice."

Introduction

The first year students are given orientation in various voluntary agencies, governmental organisations and community settings prior to their placement in the concerned agencies for the concurrent fieldwork either throughout the academic year or for a particular period. The purpose of orientation is to introduce students to the different fields of social work, different kinds of agencies, use of different techniques, methods, professional approaches and practices. Generally, the schools of social work plan orientation programmes according to the syllabi and organise visits to these agencies. However, the procedure and methods of organising visits vary from school to school. Usually, the orientation visits are organised prior to the actual placement in the agencies for concurrent fieldwork and these visits are normally completed during the first term of the year. In moffussil areas such visits are often organised casually, resulting in the students being either confused or ignorant of the nature, scope and subject matter of the orientation visits. To make the students aware of the purpose of orientation training before the placement of concurrent fieldwork practice, they should first be given the objectives of orientation. These objectives have been discussed below.

Objectives of Orientation

The major objectives of orientation training to MSW first year students are discussed in detail to enable them to understand the nature and structure of different kinds of agencies wherein the students are supposed to carry out fieldwork later throughout the academic year.

(i) To help the students know the various kinds of personal, family, professional and social problems faced by the society and to develop an understanding of society's response to these social problems through various services.
(ii) To assist the students learn the different social work techniques, methods and skills used by the workers in the respective agencies for effective solution to problems and to acquire the necessary skills and to develop a spirit of inquiry.
(iii) To make the students realise the roles to be played by them in the agencies during the fieldwork and to develop the ability to critically evaluate their roles.
(iv) To assist the students to explore the policies which they have to follow during their fieldwork training.
(v) To enable the students to know and understand the subjects or aspects covered and dealt with by the agencies.
(vi) To enable the students to know the entire field of social work and its scope for the practice of social work.
(vii) To make students realise the expectations of the schools in terms of their behaviour and performance in the agencies during the visits in concurrent fieldwork.

The orientation training is imparted to fulfil the objectives discussed above and the schools of social work should also take enough care to achieve this purpose. In order to be able to participate meaningfully in the training, students must first understand the different methods of orientation, which have been discussed below.

Methods of Orientation

The methods of orientation are discussed in detail not only for the understanding of the students but also for the schools to enable them to organise the orientation systematically and methodically.

These methods of orientation are as under:

(i) Self-study of theories of the fields of social work in general.
(ii) Scientific thinking on the theory, and understanding the fields in practice.

(iii) Introduction to the fields of social work through classroom lectures.
(iv) Professional discussions of the fields of social work with faculty members.
(v) Orientation of the concerned agencies by the faculty members to the students.
(vi) Orientation of the field practitioners to the students regarding the functioning of the agencies in general and social work in particular.
(vii) Observational understanding of the students in the agencies during the visits.
(viii) Professional interactions with the employees, inmates or beneficiaries in the agencies.
(ix) Professional joint discussions with the faculty and the agency supervisors in the agencies.

Procedure of Orientation

By the mere knowledge of the methods of orientation, the purpose of orientation will not be served. Therefore, it is necessary to discuss the procedure of orientation to enable the trainee students to learn the practical aspects in the field. In fact, the procedure as regards orientation has not been laid down anywhere in the schools of social work in the country. Naturally, therefore, the procedures presently being practised by students in their respective schools cannot be considered methodical or scientific in nature. To orient the students methodically the following procedure will be the most easy and scientific in nature:

Self-Study of Theory

The school should ask the students to read the relevant literature on the fields of social work before the orientation training starts. The necessary guidance should be given by the faculty members to find relevant literature immediately after admission or before the orientation starts. The students on their part have to be enthusiastic enough to understand as much as possible about the fields of social work. They should remember that a work well begun is half done. They should collect books from the library as per the guidance of the faculty members and go through them sincerely to learn and understand the fields of social work, its nature, scope, etc. Mere reading will not help them understand all this so easily. Reading should be followed up with extensive discussions. They should take an interest and initiative and discuss the matter with their classmates and faculty members. This would help them in understanding the concepts and fields clearly. It is always better to note down the points of discussion held with fellow students. This practice makes students remember most of the points or aspects easily.

Scientific Analysis of the Matter

After self-study of the theory on fields of social work, the next step is to think over the literature studied. In general, students never think over their own reading due to which most of the time they do not understand all the dimensions. The practice of scientific analysis of the theory and comparative analysis with the reality on the basis of general reading, general knowledge, common sense, general observation and personal experience of their earlier life will help students to understand the phenomenon practically. This will also enable students to know the different practices existing in the social system and social structure, reasons of such practices, changes in the practices, etc. On the basis of this a comparative analysis of theory and practice can be done on their own, which will enhance their knowledge and which will later be useful in learning scientific approaches at ease.

Introduction of the Fields

The faculty members should then get a feedback on the completion of "self-study of theory" and "thinking" processes from the students either orally or in writing. They must try and get an insight into the preparations and efforts taken by the students. This process would tell the faculty a great deal about the curiosity, zeal and interest that each individual student has for the course and his seriousness in choosing social work as a career. On the basis of this, general guidelines should be given to the students with a view to creating awareness in them and motivating them to develop their sincerity. After the general guidelines the faculty members should deliver lectures on the fields of social work keeping in mind particular agencies and their relation to the field of social work. The lectures should be interspersed with plenty of practical examples and experiments. The students should be given a historical review and then brought to the present position of social work fields in brief. This introduction of the fields of social work and its agencies, will be helpful in adding to their knowledge gained through earlier studies.

Later, during their first visit to the agency, the agency supervisors also brief the students. These briefings normally cover the following areas in respect to the agencies:

(i) Brief history of the trustees/director and organisation;
(ii) Nature and structure of the organisation;
(iii) Programmes and activities in general;
(iv) Staffing pattern and their functions in general;
(v) Facilities, normal services, expertise services and beneficiaries;
(vi) Sources of funds, methods of collection, etc.;
(vii) Use of social work techniques; and
(viii) Fieldwork in general.

The students on their part should jot down points during the orientation lectures by faculty supervisors, agency supervisors and also during self-study. They must then ponder over these points and prepare their own notes, which will be useful when they discuss them with the faculty members in the discussion session.

Organisation of Discussion

Most often reading and listening to lectures do not give the students a clear insight and understanding of the theory. Also they could have doubts regarding the fields of social work. To assist the students in overcoming these, the faculty members should organise a special session for an open discussion on the subject. The students should be encouraged to discuss any aspects of the fields. An open discussion, being one of the most effective methods of learning, will certainly help them understand the concepts while also clearing their doubts. Moreover, students will be able to develop the skills of communication that are so essential for the social work practice in the agency during the concurrent fieldwork training and also in their future life. During these discussions the faculty members should identify those students who either do not participate in the discussion or are very weak in expressing their views. Subsequently such students should be individually assisted and guided into becoming more active members of the group. This effort would certainly help students later on in the field.

Orientation by the Practitioners

The schools of social work also organise orientation lectures by experts and practitioners in the agencies during their visits to the respective agencies. The students are informed well in advance of such orientation lecture visits. They are also briefed before their visit to the agency about the behaviour and etiquette norms to be followed during such visits by the faculty. The faculty members also accompany the students to the agencies to help them learn the practical aspects through the rich and vivid experiences narrated by the experts in the field. Generally the experts discuss the following points:

(i) Growth of the organisation,
(ii) Devising programmes based on the objectives,
(iii) Goals achieved by the organisation,
(iv) Implementation of the fund collection drives,
(v) Professional and expertise services rendered,
(vi) Procedure of using social techniques and skills,
(vii) Impact of the services on the life pattern of the beneficiaries and on the community as a whole, and
(viii) Social changes and developments taking place due to their services.

Observation of Functions

Preparation of theory, thinking, discussions, lectures, orientation lectures, etc., helps the students understand the general background and ideas of social agencies. However, to enable them gain more practical experience, they are advised to observe the work at the micro level. The students then spend time working with the agency and the staff, observing the working procedures. This direct observation increases the students' curiosity to learn more and more of the problems of human beings and social work practice for their effective solutions. This curiosity and inquisitiveness provide the necessary impetus, and the doubts existing in their minds translate into questions during the various discussion sessions.

Purposeful Interactions

The students are asked to interact with the inmates, beneficiaries, employees and the concerned persons in the agencies to know the different aspects, which do not come to the fore in the earlier processes. This kind of purposeful interaction can be had either during the observational round or separately afterwards but before having practical dialogue with the supervisors. Interactional information provides real practical knowledge and it also helps them to develop the skills of communication, the art of conducting interviews, understanding the sufferings of people and their feelings, and in putting forth their opinions and suggestions.

General Study

Soon after observational and interactional rounds in the agencies the students are asked to give a thought to some of the general aspects that they may have come across in the agencies. This study includes their views on slogans, phrases, thoughts, photographs of great personalities displayed on the walls in the agencies and their impact over the inmates, beneficiaries, employees and the visitors' in terms of the changes these bring about in their behaviour and attitudes. This study of the general aspects enhances their knowledge and also helps to improve their observation power which will help them in future where they may work.

Dialogues on Orientation

The agency personnel and the faculty members organise a joint session to have dialogues on the orientation training in general and professional social work in particular. A free and open atmosphere is created to enable the students to have dialogues without any hesitation on any point concerned with the agencies. This method also assists the students in picking up many practical aspects. However, the initiative is totally with the students, as to how well they use this opportunity to enhance their knowledge. The loss caused due to their laziness, carelessness and inactiveness in not utilising this opportunity in spite of the fact that schools and agencies have provided these would be irrevocable.

Personal Induction

During the orientation training the students are asked to introduce themselves to the agency supervisors and the agency personnel.

With this formal introduction the orientation visits are completed. There is a vote of thanks after this. This job normally is entrusted to the students for their practice and courage.

Orientation Report

Generally, students may not be having any previous knowledge of writing a report of their study or training. The faculty member who is in charge of the training programme should ask the students to assemble on the second day of their visit in their respective schools and guide them about it. The procedure and methods of writing reports and evaluation seem to vary from school to school. However, getting the reports prepared by the students after group conference is always better because the students can collect useful information in the conference. Moreover, preparing such study reports is a new and difficult task for the fresh students. Therefore, even though they are confused about it they somehow complete the task. Such reports are normally incomplete and often the presentations vary from student to student. Taking this into consideration, a model report has been devised and discussed here for reference. These orientation reports can be written on separate sheets and submitted as a file of reports of all the visits to the schools for evaluation. Alternatively, the reports can be written in the journals. The school's instructions should be followed regarding the submission of the reports. The evaluation and allotment of the marks in front of the students is always better because it will then be possible to point out the weaknesses and strengths of the students.

Orientation Visit Report Model

General

(a) Name of the Agency :
(b) Name of the Trainee :
(c) Visit No and Report No. :
(d) Day and Date :
(e) Faculty Supervisor :
(f) Agency Supervisor :

Introduction

The orientation visit of MSW Part-I was organised by ______________ on __________ at __________ a.m./p.m.

The orientation visit is part and parcel of the concurrent fieldwork training in social work education. It is an introductory and observational visit to the social agency to understand its nature, structure, objectives, goals, activities, functions and methods of work, work culture and use of social work techniques in social work practice.

The faculty supervisor Mr. __________________________ guided us before paying the visit to the proposed agency. With this background, a visit was paid to ________________________. Mr./Mrs. __________________________, the agency supervisor welcomed us. Prof./Dr. ________________________, Faculty Supervisor, introduced the agency supervisor to our group and requested us to introduce ourselves to the agency supervisor. Accordingly, we all introduced ourselves to him/her. Then the agency supervisor gave detailed information regarding the agency and its work. We also visited and observed the different departments and their activities. The information collected from the respective personnel as well as from our observations is presented here for its evaluation.

Location of the Agency

This agency is located in ____________________ (geographical location).

Background of the Agency

_____________________________________ was established in the year _________ Mr. _______________ is/was the founder member of this agency. This agency has _________ branches in ___________state. The Head Office is situated at _____________. It is registered under ____________________ and its Registration No. is __________________. The actual functioning started in the year __________. Mr. ____________________ is the President/Chairman.

Board of Directors

(1) ____________________ Chairman/President.

(2) ____________________ Vice Chairman/Vice President.
(3) ____________________ Secretary.
(4) ____________________ Joint Secretary.
(5) ____________________ Treasurer.
(6) ____________________ Director.
(7) ____________________ Director.
(8) ____________________ Director.
(9) ____________________ Director.
(10) ____________________ Director.
(11) ____________________ Director.

Organisational Structure

Staff/designations, Job Description, etc.

Objectives of the Agency

The major objectives of the agency are:
(1)
(2)
(3)
(4)
(5)

Capital Investment

The funds have been raised from different sources, i.e., Community/Trust/Government/Foreign Funds/Personal Loan. The total capital investment required to set up this agency is/was Rs.__________. The present capital turnover is Rs.________. The agency is also getting grants from ______________________ for the ______________________.

Activities/Programmes/Production

(Explain in details)

Use of Social Work Methods

(Explain regarding casework, group work, community organisation, social welfare administration, Social work research, social action.)

Contribution of Agency

(Explain in brief)

Additional Information

Role of Social Worker
(Explain in brief)

Observation
(Explain in brief)

Remarks

Signature (Faculty Supervisor)	Signature (Student)

Common Group Conference

It is said that perception and grasping power is found more or less proportion in every human being. Naturally, the students may perceive and grasp studies as per their capacities. With this in mind, a common group conference on orientation training should be organised by the students themselves with the help of the final year students and under the guidance and control of the faculty members. The talented students who are interested in presenting their papers should be asked to share their experiences and this could be followed by discussions in a free and frank atmosphere. This will enable the students to develop their competence and capacities. Students should bear in mind that their lack of initiative may result in heavy loss for themselves and they may lag behind as a result of it. To understand the participation of the students the report of common group conference should be taken from the students. A model report has been devised for the purpose and can be referred to:

Report of Common Group Conference

(i) Name of the Student :
(ii) Name of the School :
(iii) Year and Batch No. :
(iv) Name of the Faculty in charge :
(v) Gist of the paper written on orientation training for presentation :

(vi) Participation in the seminar/ conference and the questions raised for discussions :
(vii) Supported the views/answers of the colleagues or explained answers in the seminar :
(viii) Exchange of ideas and opinions and recorded suggestions, if any :
(ix) Assisted in organising the conference/seminar :
(x) Special contribution in conference, if any :
(xi) Observations in the conference, if any :
(xii) Remarks :

Signature Supervisor/ (Faculty in charge)	Signature (Student)

Evaluation of Orientation

Schools of social work should have the practice of evaluating the orientation training imparted in the beginning, i.e., before the placement of the students for the concurrent fieldwork. This evaluation is neglected by the schools due to which the preparedness of the students cannot be understood. Yet the students are placed in the agencies for further training, i.e., concurrent fieldwork. Evaluation, after completion of this first phase, helps generate curiosity in the field, interest in particular service or activity, and the agencies where they can contribute. Schools can choose their own methods of evaluation, i.e., internal or external. However, it would be better if the experts are called in for evaluation of orientation training because this helps both the schools and the students in building up sincerity. Along with this the self-evaluation method should also be adopted. This would enable students to evaluate and judge their performances on their own. The following self-evaluation format devised for the purpose may be referred to:

Self-Evaluation Model

(i)	Name of the Student	:
(ii)	Name of the School	:
(iii)	Year and Batch No.	:
(iv)	Roll No.	:
(v)	Name of the faculty supervisor	:
(vi)	Name of the agencies and supervisors, if any	:
(vii)	Nature of the agencies	:
(viii)	Nature of the studies carried out during the visits	:
(ix)	Observation of the organisational work	:
(x)	Social aspects learnt during the visit	:
(xi)	Usefulness or utility of the orientation training for the further training	:
(xii)	Participation of student in orientation fieldwork training and process of learning	:
(xiii)	Nature of experience gained during the orientation training	:
(xiv)	Opinion of the students regarding its preparation	:
(xv)	Suggestions of the students regarding orientation training	:
(xvi)	Marks deserved	:

Signature
(Supervisor)

Signature
(Student)

Think and Do

"The novel methods and techniques of social work learnt through orientations generates curiosity in the students to practise these in agencies/field, and thereby gain a different kind of experience of life."

Chapter 4
Work with Individuals

"Sound practical knowledge of casework enhances the chances of caseworkers to identify cases in the community throughout their life and helps them to practise casework even if their chosen field is different."

Introduction

Casework is one of the direct methods of social work. It is practised in all fields of social work and helps individuals to solve their problems effectively on their own accord. Therefore, the schools of social work impart practical training to the students in casework through social welfare agencies to enhance their practical knowledge and to train them in dealing with any type of problem in the field. However, the schools, agencies and students face certain genuine problems during the process of training, like

- Non-availability of good agencies having scope for casework;
- Non-availability of trained and experienced manpower to guide the trainee casework students;
- Allotment of office work instead of casework;
- Allotment of complicated cases instead of simple ones to new and fresh students;
- Non-availability of practical curriculum; and
- Non-availability of fieldwork manual.

In spite of these handicaps, students are placed in social agencies and asked to work in the agencies throughout the academic year hoping that the agency supervisors would give them cases later. But most of the time it so happens that for the whole academic year is wasted in the students waiting for allotment of a case for study. Such students are deprived of casework practice and instead, end their fieldwork training doing the agency's office work.

The schools of social work in moffussil areas accept this helplessly and also issue certificates of completion of training. This situation also forces the students to remain silent because of the internal grading systems.

Taking into an account the pathetic condition of casework training, an attempt has been made to explain the procedure and practice of casework, to enable students to do casework on their own without any difficulty either in the agency or outside the agency. Casework can be taken up whenever and wherever they come across any client or affected people, either during the training period or after completion of the training period. To do so the students should know the general and specific objectives of training in casework otherwise they will not be able to understand its core.

Objectives of Training in Casework

The following objectives of casework training are to be studied carefully and understood. The conceptual clarity of these in a professional sense will enable the students to grasp the core of casework technique. This is possible only when the students put in sincere efforts and follow the proper methodology of self-study.

- To provide an opportunity to the students to study the nature, scope, extension and magnitude of casework practices in different fields of social work.
- To enable the students to understand the application of casework principles in practice.
- To assist students to study the process of casework, to study ways of diagnosing problems, preparing treatment plans and evaluating casework practices.
- To help students to learn the interviewing process in casework practice and the principles, techniques and skills to be used for interviewing clients and concerned people.
- To enable students to prepare casework records for practical use.
- To provide an opportunity for students to understand preventive and curative process in casework.
- To enable the students to develop the required skills, to use casework techniques in the Indian culture.

Methods of Self-Study

The following methods of self-study are suggested for better comprehension and help in applying theoretical aspects to practical use:

(i) Theoretical preparation before doing practicals.
(ii) Scientific thinking of the theory and the facts.
(iii) Professional discussion with the faculty members.
(iv) Professional interaction with the inmates or clients.
(v) Study of case studies recorded in journals and case files.
(vi) Observation of casework process and practice in the agency.
(vii) Professional discussion with the agency supervisors.
(viii) Casework practice or handling the cases personally.

Students are required to go through the relevant literature pertaining to casework especially social work concepts, philosophy, social work skills, principles and components of casework, etc. Without reading this literature it will not be possible for them to execute practical work in the field. The faculty members may not be in a position to teach and explain this literature in classrooms, in the beginning of the academic year or at the time of placement of students for casework. This does not mean that the students should wait for classroom lectures to be completed on the subject. Students can request their faculty supervisors to orient them on casework theory in brief, if not in detail. Self-preparation and brief orientation will help them to understand the concepts clearly. This is essential as otherwise the students are not welcomed in their respective agencies. It may also have an adverse effect on their evaluation. More serious is the damage a lack of preparation will cause in terms of the quality of learning they will get and students may end up learning casework but not with a professional attitude.

Theoretical preparation always helps students to learn the nature of casework in general, but to understand it thoroughly students will have to think and refer to the theory to correlate facts. Such comparative analytical study of theory and facts will give birth to new ideas and creativity. Therefore, this process should be practised by the students throughout the academic year, whenever they find time. Such practices will enable the students to learn different dimensions of individual problems and casework. Not only should a comparative analytical study of theory and facts be undertaken but students should also probe deeper and try to get an insight into the social system and social structure existing earlier and methods used for solving problems of individuals, if these solutions still hold true in the changed social structure, etc. For example, answers to questions like what was the nature of individual problems; why are the earlier social institutions like joint family system, caste panchayat, etc., ineffective today to solve the individual problems in the changing society; whether this new American method–casework–is suitable and useful in the changing Indian culture; what is the scope for casework practice in different fields of social work; what are the skills required to be developed to make this method effective and scientific; should be sought.

Constant reading of the available literature, scientific pondering over the theory and facts, comparative analyses of theory and facts, evolving new methods of solving individual problems, etc., increases the level of understanding of the students. But certain concepts, terms, process, procedure and practices may not be clear to them. So, to get these concepts clear it is necessary to have professional discussions with the faculty members who will explain the concepts, illustrating examples of casework practices in America where casework was devised and developed. The different aspects learnt through discussions with the faculty members may help the students to get a clear picture of casework.

However, even a clear understanding of casework theory may not be enough to understand the multi-dimensional casework practice. Other methods like professional interaction should also be used to learn the practical aspects. Therefore, professional interaction with experienced casework practitioners, chronic patients, clients, etc., will enable students to learn certain typical incidences and cases, and such informative studies may add to their knowledge. This preparation will give self-confidence to the students because the more they read and study past cases, the more they shall be equipped to handle cases on their own. Certain case studies reported in professional magazines or cases in the files of the agencies should be studied sincerely. These will help the students to develop the required skills of handling cases on their own.

With this theoretical preparation students should observe physical handling or dealing of some cases by either the agency supervisors where they are posted or some professional practitioners. They will then get an idea of casework process and procedure in a practical sense. This observation by the students will help them assess the entire process. A lot is learnt when theoretical concepts are sound and one sees this theory being put to practice. This coordinated procedure also helps students to retain in their memory the problem at hand, the way the case was handled and the solution given. The students should discuss with the caseworkers in the agencies and find out about the following facts:

- follow-up process,
- acceptance of the clients,
- clients development.

The general information as regards the follow-up, client's development and relevant facts may help the students to add to their knowledge. Moreover, it is necessary to know as much of this technique as is available and possible. Therefore, the students should know about earlier cases: (i) whether clients overcame their weakness and developed their self-confidence, (ii) whether the clients were able to develop their personalities, and (iii) whether the clients were accepted by their families and their communities. Such information will help them understand the utility of casework practice. This general fieldwork information enables the students to be sound in theory before doing fieldwork or casework in social work education. Moreover, it makes them able and competent enough to handle the cases. This does not mean that they can solve all the cases or problems easily because the nature of cases may not be similar every time. Fieldwork study should be reported to the concerned faculty supervisor in the format prescribed for the purpose.

Report of General Casework

(i) Name of the student :
(ii) Name of the school :
(iii) Year and Batch No. :
(iv) Class and Roll No. :
(v) Literature studied on casework :
(vi) Nature of information collected during this period :

(vii) Methods used for the general fieldwork :
(viii) Guidance and cooperation of the faculty and agency supervisors :
(ix) Utility value of general fieldwork knowledge for casework practice :
(x) Problems and difficulties faced during the general fieldwork :
(xi) Opinions and suggestions regarding general fieldwork :
(xii) Marks deserved :

Remarks:

Signature (Faculty)

Signature (Student)

Allotment of Cases

After rigorous fieldwork on casework practices in the agencies and gaining sufficient practical knowledge to deal with the cases individually, the students should request the agency supervisors to allot some simple cases for study and practice. The students should observe societal norms in the premises of the agencies and interact with the clients in a professional sense. They should also bear in mind that certain practices relating to regularity, punctuality, discipline and morality influence people and institutional culture.

Fieldwork to be done hereafter for handling the cases in social work perspective has its own methods, techniques and skills.

Casework Procedure

Casework students should request the agency supervisors to allow them to go through the personal files of the clients allotted to them for handling the cases. This request to go through the files may or may not be considered by the agency. However, in cases where the request is denied students generally get confused and rush to the faculty supervisors for help. In fact, casework students should learn skills of managing such affairs and elicit or solicit cooperation of the agency personnel on their own. This will help them learn administrative qualities. Due and sincere efforts should be put in by the students to achieve the required cooperation. However, in spite of their sincere efforts if they do not get co-operation, they must approach the faculty supervisors asking for their intervention. These files should be studied carefully to understand the background of the clients through case sheets, observational notes and other relevant information contained therein. Generally the background information recorded in the case sheets are as under:

Case Sheet

Personal Data

(i) Name of the client :
(ii) Address :
(iii) Age :
(iv) Sex :
(v) Education :
(vi) Religion and sub-caste :
(vii) Hobbies :
(viii) Habits :
(ix) Nature of problem :
(x) Background of the case :
(xi) Admission in the agency :
(xii) Police or agency report :
(xiii) Parents' background in terms of education, economy, occupation, attitudes and approaches, etc. :
(xiv) General background of the family :

Signature
(Superintendent)

Once the case sheets are studied carefully the students will have an idea about the nature of the case which will form the base for their further interventional inquiry. With this general background study the process of casework practice starts with professional interaction.

Induction of the Clients

To begin with, the casework students should be introduced to the clients. A formal introduction helps the students to interact with the clients and to initiate the process of establishing rapport and professional relationship. Once a relationship is established and strengthened the students will be able to understand the introvert and extrovert personalities of the clients. Such understanding is called professional induction of the clients. For this, students will have to spend sufficient time and put in lot of efforts. However, some of the students are not able to do this and get stuck at this stage for a long period. To overcome this problem the students must recall their experiences in establishing relationships with their friends and a similar method should be applied to establish a rapport. Generally, discussing the likes, dislikes and interests of the client creates a favourable atmosphere for interaction. So casework students can initiate a dialogue with their clients on similar lines and make them feel free to express their feelings about their own likes and interests. Such attempts will be useful to develop an affinity and to establish a bond. There is a possibility that the clients may establish an emotional relation with the casework students. However, the students must strictly stick to a professional relationship and not an emotional one because the latter may not be fruitful in the professional sense. The professional relationship becomes the base for casework process which helps the students enhance the self-confidence of the clients which makes them pour their heart out.

Professional Interactions with the Client

Establishment of rapport and enhancing the confidence of the clients in the beginning helps casework students to create a favourable atmosphere to start the actual process of the casework. However, the students should be careful and bear in mind that direct questions should be avoided during the process of interview, as in any business interviews. The formalities of conducting interviews with the clients should be avoided, however, certain principles like privacy should be practised consciously. The atmosphere in the place of interview should be such that the clients should not feel like they are being interviewed. The interviews should take place in a very natural atmosphere otherwise clients may not express their feelings and may not narrate their woes openly. Similarly, casework students should always keep in mind that clients are also intelligent. They could hide real facts easily and narrate cooked up stories to create confusion and make the caseworker believe them. Therefore, it is necessary to remember and record what is said so as to cross-examine clients when they are interviewed again for the same purpose. Such notes will also help in comparative analysis of client's statements with those of other persons concerned, to know and to judge the exact truth. Sometimes, the clients speak out everything they have in their minds and this is possible only when they feel that the casework students are genuinety their helpers friends, and enablers, and they practise the principle of confidentiality.

Collection of Information from the Parents

The information collected from the clients through a series of interviews may be inadequate, untrue, false or cooked up and so it may not be sufficient to draw correct conclusions about the exact cause of the problem so as to diagnose the suffering. Therefore, sufficient information should be collected from other sources like clients, parents, neighbours, friends and relatives. Such information will definitely assist caseworkers in making the correct perfect diagnosis. But the casework students should be aware that the parents of the clients might not give their responses so easily because of fear or mistrust. Necessary skills, techniques, methods, i.e., effective communication, art of building an image and penetrating rehabilitative interventions, in the minds of the parents will help the students to learn different dimensions of the problem. The information collected from the parents should also be recorded in the casework diaries in their own words so that those words can be interpreted properly afterwards which will assist them in drawing the right conclusions.

Collection of Information from Neighbours

Human beings are social animals and always live and move in the community. The neighbourhood is the first social community in which a person lives. Naturally neighbours know many things about people who reside in the vicinity. The personal observations of the neighbours from different angles and perspectives are necessary to understand the personalities of the clients, and their problems and the situations responsible for them. Therefore, the casework students should conduct interviews with the neighbours for the purpose of gaining a better insight into the lives of clients. However, they should be conscious of two very important aspects: first, the remarks could be biased with malintentions, and second, they could be misleading if the respondents fear possibilities of quarrels arising as a direct result of their partaking in the interview process involving persons beyond their families. It is essential to clear such doubts, if any, in their minds, by explaining the objectives of the interviews in a friendly manner. The information collected from the neighbours should also be recorded in the diaries in their own words.

Collection of Information from Friends, Relatives and Teachers

Relevant information, events, facts and responsible situations and conditions regarding the problems of the clients should also be collected from friends, relatives and teachers. First, these people must be taken into confidence, their doubts should be cleared and the objectives of the interviews should be explained. The responses of the concerned people should be recorded in their own words for proper interpretation and analysis to finally make the diagnosis.

Discussion with Supervisors

Once information is collected from the concerned individuals through a series of interviews and correspondence, the data collected should be interpreted for the right meaning and the responsible causes or set of causes should be arrived at. After this interpretation and preliminary conclusions regarding the reasons, the caseworkers should discuss the matter with the agency as well as with the faculty supervisors to confirm their diagnosis. It is to be remembered that the diagnosis has to be correct otherwise the treatment given would be useless and their effort, time and money will go waste. More serious is the consequences such wrong diagnosis will bring in terms of the harm it will bring to the agency's reputation, and could result in the agency turning down further requests of schools for placement of their students for casework in social work education.

Treatment Plan

It is often very difficult to prepare a proper treatment plan and if trainee students are confused it would make it that much more difficult. To be able to prepare a good treatment plan requires sound knowledge, a wide social outlook, perspective, imagination, logical power and judgement. This, however, does not mean that it is an impossible task. The casework students should try to recall in their memory experiences and situations of similar kinds. The following example may clear the concepts of diagnosis. Whenever a patient goes to the doctor and says that he is suffering from temperature, the doctor will not give him medicine just because the patient says so. He checks the patient, inquires and looks for symptoms and judges the exact cause. Only then does he gives medicines. Similarly, the treatment plan in casework should also be prepared and expert help should be taken. In casework the clients should not be asked to take a particular decision to solve their problems. A favourable atmosphere should be created to help them make their own decisions to solve their problems.

Follow-Up

Expertise services rendered according to the treatment plan will definitely help the clients in bringing necessary changes in their personalities, which in turn, create confidence in them. This self-confidence gained through the agency services helps them to solve their problems. Once the problems are solved clients can resume their normal lives. However, students should always follow-up their cases and find out about the progress and development of their clients from time to time. Normally, students do not observe this practice because they stop going to the agencies after the end of the academic year. Being professionals they should practise follow-ups, even if the academic year ends, either by paying personal visits to the residences of the clients or through correspondence with the clients directly or through the agencies. Collecting information regarding the development of the clients whom they have helped will definitely bring happiness to their hearts and will give one a feeling of having been of some use to the society.

Evaluation of Casework

The students are supposed to evaluate the entire process of casework they practised during the period of training and try to judge if they used the social work skills and techniques properly to achieve the objectives and goals, whether the clients have come out of their problems, whether their skills developed as students in the process, whether they have learnt the art of dealing with clients, etc. Such a process, self-evaluation will help them to make out their weakness and will help them overcome these in future to perform better casework practice on scientific lines. The casework report should be submitted to the agency and the school, for record and evaluation. The format devised for the purpose may be referred to for preparation of the report.

Model of Report on Completion of Case

(i) Name of the student :
(ii) Name of the school :
(iii) Batch number :
(iv) Roll number :
(v) Name of the client and address :
(vi) Background of the client in brief :
(vii) Nature of their problem :
(viii) Casework study and practice in brief :
(ix) Failure or success in solving the case with reasons :
(x) Reporting to the agency :
(xi) Opinions and suggestions :

Day: Signature
Date: (Student)
Place:
Remarks:

Signature (Agency Supervisor) Signature (Faculty Supervisor)

Instructions to the Students

According to casework procedure the students should help the individuals and solve minimum five different types of cases during the academic year. However, in case of technical difficulties at least one case may be solved during the academic year. Solving the case means that an amicable solution is arrived at. For example, in case of marital conflicts it is not necessary that the solution is that both husband and wife should live together at any cost. If there are genuine difficulties in living under one roof, separation may be the only amicable solution. Generally it is expected that students should be able to understand the stages of casework process in its right sense even if they have not been able to solve the case/s despite their sincere efforts.

Send-off Programme

The agency supervisors and the office employees impart training to the students throughout the academic year without any remuneration. Though it is their social responsibility the time, labour and efforts taken by them should be appreciated and the students must have a sense of gratitude for them. For this, a special programme should be organised to thank them. The contribution of the agency supervisors and the experts should always be acknowledged. Their addresses should be collected and recorded in the personal diaries for communication in future. The students should inform their supervisors of their professional development every now and then. Such communication and will give pleasure and happiness to the agency supervisors which may help them in changing their attitudes and approach towards fieldwork training, and the future students to come will get welcome cooperation, sufficient information as well as sincere guidance. It will also help the schools of social work to establish cordial relations with the concerned agencies.

Annual Fieldwork Seminar

After the send-off programme in the agencies the students should organise a fieldwork seminar in their respective schools to present their cases and share their experiences gained during casework studies and casework practices. Experts may be invited to this seminar for their guidance and suggestions. The students should organise this seminar under the guidance of the faculty supervisors. The seminar reports should be submitted to the concerned faculty supervisors. The formats devised for the purpose may be referred to for preparing their report.

Model of Report on Fieldwork Seminar

(i) Name of the student :
(ii) Name of the school :
(iii) Batch number :
(iv) Roll Number :
(v) Theme of annual fieldwork seminar :
(vi) No. of days :
(vii) Paper presentations :
(viii) Role of the students in organisation, presentation participation :
(ix) Skills and methods used for organising seminar :
(x) Response of the students, colleagues and their participation :
(xi) Problems and difficulties in organising the seminar :
(xii) Cooperation of the supervisors :
(xiii) Opinions and suggestions :

Remarks:

Signature (Faculty) Signature (Student)

Self-Evaluation

It is said that self-evaluation is the best evaluation. Students should assess their own performances on the basis of what they have learnt in the field and the efforts they have taken to complete their casework training. The evaluation should be done honestly and the report submitted to the concerned faculty supervisors for their evaluation. The format devised for the purpose may be referred to for preparing the self-evaluation report.

Self-Evaluation Report

(i)	Name of the student	:
(ii)	Name of the school	:
(iii)	Batch number	:
(iv)	Roll number	:
(v)	Name of the faculty supervisor	:
(vi)	Name of the agency supervisor	:
(vii)	Duration of placement	:
(viii)	Nature of general study as regards agency	:
(ix)	No. of cases handled	:
(x)	Social work skills and methods used to handle the cases	:
(xi)	Use of innovative ideas to deal with the cases	:
(xii)	Performance in the field	:
(xiii)	Opinions regarding the guidance sought from the faculty and the agency supervisors	:
(xiv)	Administrative assignments for study	:

Signature
(Student)

Remarks:

Place:
Date:

Signature
(Faculty)

Recording: Casework Diary

In general the students of first year in moffussil areas are found lacking skills of writing diaries due to which they are confused when it comes to writing casework diaries. Their traditional writing style is restricted to mentioning the visit numbers, time, and one or two sentences about their visits and return. In fact, students should avoid writing the formalities every time and diaries should be written in brief only about the work done by them. They could refer to Chapter I to understand the purpose of writing casework diaries and journals which will enable them to understand the method of writing diaries. A few models have been illustrated here as examples.

Examples of Casework Diaries

1

Visit No.:
Day:
Date:

The first fieldwork visit was an introductory visit. So my co-fieldwork colleagues and I introduced ourselves to the agency supervisors. The agency supervisor also introduced himself and briefed us about his personal, educational and service background along with general information regarding his induction into the agency. This introduction was done in a friendly manner but it taught us the etiquette and manners of introduction with officers. After this, all the fieldwork students placed in that agency went inside the office, got acquainted with the other office employees.

Signature (Agency Supervisor)	Signature (Faculty Supervisor)	Signature (Student)

2

Visit No.:
Day:
Date:

The agency supervisors asked me to collect general information regarding the agency from the office staff to know the nature and structure of the agency. Accordingly I met all the concerned employees and collected information, i.e., establishment, registration number, trustees, constitution, objectives, goals achieved by the agency, etc.

Signature (Agency Supervisor)	Signature (Faculty Supervisor)	Signature (Student)

3

Visit No.:
Day:
Date:

Today I was asked to observe the functioning of the agency. So I sat in the office and observed the manner, etiquette, style of speaking, language used, the subjects dealt with, and the nature of the work they do in the office of the agency.

Signature (Agency Supervisor)	Signature (Faculty Supervisor)	Signature (Student)

4

Visit No.:
Day:
Date:

After a general study made in the agency in four visits, I was asked to go through the files of some case studies. As per the instructions, I went through a few of the case files and understood the contents, drafting, language, presentation, procedure, nature of the problems of the clients and the way of handling the cases by the agency supervisors. This helped me to get a general idea about casework.

Signature (Agency Supervisor)	Signature (Faculty Supervisor)	Signature (Student)

5

Visit No.:
Day:
Date:

To understand the handling of the cases I was asked to observe the casework practice in the agency in three or four visits. Accordingly I sat before the agency supervisor and observed the dealings, i.e., skills of the social caseworker.

Signature (Agency Supervisor)	Signature (Faculty Supervisor)	Signature (Student)

6

Visit No.:
Day:
Date:

The preliminary studies gave me an idea of doing casework practice. So I requested the supervisor to allot me a simple case. Considering my self-confidence, a case has been allotted to me for study and practice.

Signature (Agency Supervisor)	Signature (Faculty Supervisor)	Signature (Student)

7

Visit No.:
Day:
Date:

After getting preliminary information about the case from the file and background information from the agency supervisors I decided to conduct interviews of the client to unearth the facts of the case for helping her. Accordingly I interviewed the client today and got certain information about her marital conflicts.

Signature (Agency Supervisor)	Signature (Faculty Supervisor)	Signature (Student)

Journal Writing

The students attending schools of social work located in rural areas are normally confused about writing the journal of casework, i.e., whether to write journals visit-wise or case-wise and secondly, how to write the cases. Due to lack of proper guidance they are not able to cultivate the habit of writing journals systematically. The following model may help them to write journals on their own and help them learn the skills of writing and presenting the cases and ideas.

Model of Casework Journal

Agency	:
Agency Supervisor	:
Faculty Supervisor	:
Visit Numbers	:
Client	: Mrs. Kamal.

Background of the Case

Mrs. Kamal is a 25 year old woman, working as a school faculty in Solapur city. She got the job a year ago and she has been married for the past two years. She belongs to the Hindu religion and has married a person of her own religion and caste. Her husband is also educated and is working in the same profession as a school faculty in a nearby village. Both were living happily in a house, which they own, for the last two years until recently when she got the job. From then on Mrs. Kamal noticed a change in her husband's (Mr. Prakash) behaviour and their personal life has gone sour. Both are leveling charges against each other.

Preliminary Study

The background of the above case was studied carefully. A thorough reading from the case file of the agency was made. Certain information was collected from the agency supervisors and office employees. After collecting as much detail as possible the caseworker thought over the entire case to understand the logical reason of their not getting along well. Considering that the couple was happy initially in the two years of married life, and the fact that things started changing after this period, a preliminary conclusion was that this was a case of the honeymoon roses. It was inferred that the cause could be that the nature and behaviour of the two did not match. Initially as the marriage was new things did not seem so evident. However, with passing of time either could not stand the other's nature. With this preliminary conclusion about the cause of the problem the caseworker started dealing with the client.

First Meeting

During the first meeting she was very silent. This was natural because she was meeting the caseworker, a virtual stranger, for the first time. She did not know anything about the caseworker. Normally no one would like to discuss personal problems with unknown people. Being the first visit the caseworker decided to only introduce him to her, to make her feel that the caseworker was her friend, philosopher and enabler. Generally, friendship cannot be developed in one or two meetings but to begin with one has to try to make the other feel that he is interested in being a friend. Friendship develops on the basis of nature, like-mindedness, interests, feelings, positive attitudes, good approaches and the like. So, to strike a relation of friendship with her the caseworker decided to understand her interests, likes and dislikes. All efforts were put in by the caseworker to create a cordial atmosphere and the caseworker managed to create a feeling of assurance in her. Slowly interaction was initiated and she began to open up. At the end of the session though she seemed to have some doubts about, the caseworker, the latter was pretty confident that he had struck a chord in her somewhere along the line and the caseworker could see friendly relations starting to develop.

Second Meeting

In the second meeting she was looking fresh and was waiting for the caseworker to come to the agency. The caseworker was very happy to see this and got additional confidence. This was a sign of acceptance as a friend and enabler. Taking this opportunity the caseworker decided to continue the same topics of discussion to which she had responded positively. During the course of this discussion the caseworker could observe that she expected appreciation of her good deeds which she had done in her family earlier. The caseworker immediately appreciated her achievements sincerely. She responded by showing her delight and started opening up further. Slowly she started expressing her sorrows. She wanted that somebody listens to her sorrows. The caseworker obliged with a sincere and professional approach. Her feelings were understood and to reassure her the caseworker said, "Please do not worry, wait, God will mete out justice because you have done so many good things". She was very happy to know that somebody was listening to her.

Third Meeting

She had understood by this time that the caseworker came to the agency twice a week and from the agency the caseworker come to her house. The caseworker always found her waiting for him on these days. This eagerness indicated that she was interested in solving her problems. It was only during the third meeting that she opened up the topic of her personal and family life and started discussing it. While discussing her marital life she expressed her feelings of being very happy with her husband and narrated some happy events and then became emotional and silent for a moment. She also recalled some of the sour events and narrated them with tears in her eyes and started blaming her fate. The caseworker supported her by consoling her and asked her to wait for some time because time was the only healer in such cases. She believed it and requested, "Please do something to set things right". This indicated that she still wanted their marriage to work out. After listening to her, the caseworker decided to meet the parents and other family members. The address of her parents was collected for the purpose.

Interview with the Parents

According to the plan a visit was paid to her parents' home and the caseworker met them in connection with the problem. They happily welcomed him. To begin with, it was necessary to understand their social background and family culture. This information was collected in a casual discussion, which helped the caseworker to discuss relevant and specific points, to establish friendly relations and also to create a free and frank atmosphere, which the caseworker managed. In such an atmosphere the delicate and sensitive issue of their daughter's problem was broached. Though they spoke in favour of their daughter the caseworker got a feeling that in the problem that existed they felt their daughter to be at fault. They wanted to correct this, however, they wanted somebody to help them convince her husband to forgive her and to accept her as a life partner again because they had not been able to do so on their own. Their acceptance of intervention and feeding of factual information helped the caseworker move ahead.

Interviews with Neighbours

Since the parents had indirectly blamed their own daughter for her problems and since the daughter was blaming her husband and not ready to accept her mistakes, the caseworker decided to learn if the parents were simply accepting the mistakes of their daughter to settle the matter or if their daughter was really at fault. The caseworker felt that the interviews with the neighbours were very essential at this point. A series of interviews were conducted to know the observations of the neighbours about the client's nature. After taking a lot of efforts and use of social work skills like communication, information was collected and there was again a confirmation of the parents' indirect confession of their daughter's nature and behaviour.

Interviews with Relatives

The parents' and neighbors' interviews had indicated that the nature of the client was whimsical and she was at fault. This was evident though it was not told directly. So it was necessary to know more about her nature to confirm if she was at fault. The nearest relatives were interviewed for the purpose. Due to fear the relatives too were not ready to reveal anything about their observations but somehow with the help of social work skills, rapport was established in a short period, and they acknowledged that that the client had changed after she got a job. This opinion was supported by the indirect expressions of the views of the parents and neighbours. After collecting sufficient information about the case it was decided to meet the client once again for a purposeful interaction.

Fourth Meeting with the Client

During this meeting she was more frank with the casework student than earlier. This frankness had developed because of frequent personal visits of the caseworker and the hope that she saw in getting some solutions to her problems. In this situation the casework student tried to cross-examine her changed behaviour. However, she was not ready to accept that the problem was because of her. This was all done through indirect communication of cross-examination. So once again it was decided to contact her nearest associates, especially school friends and colleagues in the school for a fact-finding study.

Interviews with Friends

A series of interviews of her close school friends and colleagues was conducted using the skills of social work. She was in touch with them in her day-to-day life, and therefore, they were having their own assessments of her nature and behaviour. All the friends expressed their feelings that she was a bit whimsical, and had changed her behaviour after getting the job and after her marriage, however, nobody pointed this out directly. At this stage, it was confirmed that she was at fault and therefore, the cause of the problem was her own nature.

Interviews with Husband

After conducting a series of interviews with the close associates around the client (Mrs. Kamal) and drawing conclusions about the case, her husband was contacted because he was the one who was very close and directly concerned with the case. In the beginning he was not ready to meet the caseworker in connection with the case. He was seen very annoyed. The caseworker was worried about his reluctance. However, after some pondering on this issue, guidance was sought from the agency and faculty supervisors. Under their guidance the caseworker met the client's husband and requested him to spare just half an hour. Due to repeated requests he agreed to do so. There was not sufficient time to establish relations to make him feel comfortable and free but only because of the art of good communication it was possible to create a rapport with him. The first expression of the caseworker, however, broke the ice and that was: "Your wife seems to be whimsical." He then narrated different incidences and events of his wife's whimsical doings and unpardonable behaviour. The thought came to the mind of the caseworker as to how one sentence against this man's wife could draw a positive response from him. To understand more of his behaviour, few of his friends were contacted for the purpose.

Interviews with the Husband's Friends

Interviews with the husband's friends were conducted to gain an insight into the husband's behaviour. From these it was understood that all his friends blamed him for his marital problem though he was not at fault. And it was due to this that the husband had gone into a shell and would not discuss the matter with anyone. However, when he found that the caseworker had a corresponding view matching that of his, he opened up, and therefore the change in attitude. After conducting interviews of all the concerned persons a conclusion was drawn. The main cause of the marital conflict between the client and her husband was her whimsical nature and the changes in her behaviour and attitudes after she got the job. This was the diagnosis.

Diagnosis of the Case

It was diagnosed that the client was responsible for the problem. The main cause was her whimsical nature and change in her behaviour after she got the job. After concluding the exact reason it was decided to prepare a plan of treatment for effective solution of the problem. This was a bit tough because knowledge of social sciences and social work was necessary and the caseworker had limitations on this front. So the faculty and agency supervisors were consulted for further guidance in preparing the treatment plan.

Plan of Treatment

Generally, problems of marital conflicts are solved by caste panchayats, voluntary social workers, etc., but their methods are different. Most of the times they exert pressure on the couple, forcing them and their family members to settle the cases under threats of social boycott. But such solutions are not scientific because the concerned persons may settle the issues due to pressures and not due to their own understanding. After some time their problems may come up again due to which their life may be ruined. Therefore, such problems should be solved effectively. To solve such problems scientifically, methods and techniques of social work should be used methodically and skillfully. Considering this, a proper treatment plan was to be prepared under the able guidance of the supervisors and on the basis of the diagnosis. In this case it was necessary to render marital counselling services till such a time that a positive change comes about in the behaviour and attitudes of both concerned. Also this counselling was required to create a favourable atmosphere as both, the client and the husband, were interested in arriving at an amicable solution to the problem. In other words, both were willing to come together once again and to lead their life together.

Marital Counselling

Being an unmarried person it was very difficult for the caseworker to counsel the concerned in connection with martial conflicts. Therefore, before starting counselling services sufficient number of books were read and the matter was discussed with the faculty and the agency supervisors. The difficulty in counselling on marital issues was therefore taken care of with this reading and with the guidance of faculty and agency supervisors. The related issues and concepts were understood and counselling sessions were planned. Counselling services were rendered for several months. The required changes were effected in the personalities of both and a favourable atmosphere was created with the help of social work skills, methods and techniques for congenial living. The client (wife) understood that she should not be so indifferent and whimsical just because she earns and is able to look after herself without support of the husband and parents. Finally, the issue was settled amicably.

Follow-up

Though it was necessary to have a follow-up programme, it was not possible for the caseworker because the training programme was time-bound. Moreover, sufficient time should lapse after the solution has been given, to observe the development and only then follow-up programmes must be initiated.

Think and Do

> *"Identifying at least one client in your life-time and helping him or her to help himself or herself in the real sense can be called as utilisation of professional knowledge for the betterment of the community."*

Chapter 5

Work with Groups

> *"Group work teaches the art of observation of actions and reactions of the members and its significance in the development of personality through group life."*

Introduction

Students of first year are placed in different voluntary organisations for group work practice, where they learn group work techniques in practical situations and render services to the agency members and to the concerned agencies. This training-cum-service is very useful to the group members, agencies and the schools of social work. However, neither the agencies nor schools are sincere enough to utilise these services for the purpose. This training, therefore, is neglected in comparison to casework. The trainee students sometimes harbour wrong notions about group work practice. Most often, conducting of different games is considered as group work. This is mainly because of the lack of interest among students, supervisors, non-availability of practical syllabus and group work manual, time adjustment problems of the agencies, etc. Yet, students are placed in the agencies year after year for group work training which is completed as yet another formality to obtain a degree. There has been no interest to assess the loss due to this and who exactly is at the losing end. The analysis of cost of training is also not done. Considering the conditions of group work training in the schools of social work especially in the rural areas and its significance from the point of view of profession and utility, a specific practical syllabus is to be framed and a work manual is to be developed by the universities.

The author here has made an attempt to prepare group work

programmes and to lay down the procedures to enable the students to understand and practice group work in its true sense.

Before proceeding to the actual group work programmes and procedures, the students must know the objectives of group work training so as to understand its nature, scope, extent and magnitude.

Objectives of Group Work

The major objectives of group work training and services are as under:

- To provide an opportunity to students to learn to form a group in the agencies during the fieldwork as well as in their respective fields of social work in future.
- To enable the students to learn and understand group work processes practically to make use of these in future.
- To help the students to do group work and to be able to diagnose the weaknesses of the members so as to develop their personalities in a group and to prepare a proper treatment plan to help the group members to overcome their weaknesses and thereby to evaluate the group.
- To assist the students to learn different techniques and skills required for group work practice, and to use them in their respective fields in future.
- To provide an opportunity to the students to prepare programmes of group work on the basis of interest of the group members and need of the group.
- To enable the students to learn to record group work practices for evaluation as well as reference and record.
- To assist the students to learn to make use of group work practices in their respective fields on scientific lines.

Induction of the Group Work Agency

(i) History of the agency,
(ii) Field of social work,
(iii) Funds and staffing pattern,
(iv) Programmes and activities,
(v) Methods or techniques,
(vi) Contribution and evaluation, and
(vii) Planning and developmental schemes.

The information pertaining to the agency can be collected from the office employees, field staff and the social workers with the help of discussions, observations and from the relevant records. Collected records should be studied carefully to understand the efforts taken, by the agency personnel and the founders, to achieve the targets or the goals of the agencies, and how their services are utilised by the beneficiaries and community at large. To understand their success, scientific approach and methodology of work, etc., a professional discussion should be held with the social workers and the founders. Their problems and difficulties should be studied and the way these were overcome should be explored. After the background study of the agency, necessary report should be prepared and added in the organisational visits diary and be recorded in the journal meant for this purpose.

Group Work Programme Planning

The group work programmes for the academic year should be planned on the basis of the objectives of group work and need of the agency, under the guidance of the faculty and agency supervisors. The students may not be able to prepare the programmes on their own and sometimes they may be confused. Therefore, the following model group work programme chart may be referred to.

Model of Group Work Programme Chart

(i) Formation of Group:

(ii) Induction of Group Members:

(a) Personal data: Collection of information regarding their age, education, caste, religion, hobbies, interest, habits, achievements, scholastic progress and drawbacks.

(b) Family data: Collection of information regarding their family background, size of the family, parents' occupation, education, earnings, comforts, facilities, family difficulties, problems and such information for application of casework practice, if necessary.

(iii) Conducting Sports:

Conduction of interesting indoor and outdoor games like *kabaddi, khokho, langadi, carom, chess,* and other such games, and work like preparation of articles, materials, etc.

(iv) Discourse or *Sanskar* Programmes:
Arranging short story narrations, songs, street plays, poems, phrases and the like, which communicate certain messages to the group members for their socialisation, development and for imbibing good values or *sanskars.*

(v) Conducting Test on General Studies:
Conducting essay competitions, elocution competitions, handwriting competitions, drawing competitions, games for vocabulary development, prize distribution programmes, etc.

(vi) Celebration of National Festivals:
Independence day celebrations, Republic day celebrations, Id, Holi, Diwali, etc.

(vii) Celebration of Anniversaries of Great Personalities:
Vinoba Bhave's Anniversary, Mahatma Gandhi's Anniversary, Lal Bahadur Shastri's Anniversary, Pandit Jawaharlal Nehru's Anniversary, Jaiprakash Narayan's Anniversary, Subhash Chandra Bose's Anniversary, Dr. Babasaheb Ambedkar's Anniversary, Shaheed Bhagat Singh's Anniversary.

(viii) Organisation of Cultural Programmes:
Arranging cultural programmes like singing, dancing, mimicry, *antakshari*, picnics, etc.

(ix) Conducting Parents Meet:
Organising or calling a meeting of the parents to have a dialogue with them for creating awareness about their children's weakness, interests, strengths, habits, hobbies, socio-psychological needs and their responsibilities in the development process.

(x) Guidance and Counselling Services:
Guidance regarding the significance of education, reading, writing, evil impact of bad habits on their life, evil impact of television, cinema, observation of social norms, cultural values and beliefs, etc.

(xi) Organising `Send-off' Programmes:
Lectures, sharing the experiences of the group members, group photographs, prizes for their contribution and participation in the group's activities and organising a farewell of the group.

(xii) Exit Interviews:
To find out the impressions of group members, their opinions

and suggestions, about the utility of group work programmes and improvement, etc.

Group Work Practice

After preparing group work programme it is necessary to prepare a time schedule on the basis of the total possible visits and the hours available during the academic year. This must be planned with the guidance of faculty and agency supervisors. Group work practice should be followed accordingly. While practising group work students should remember that they must seek the guidance of the faculty and agency supervisors for every activity on the fieldwork days. Otherwise they may not understand the need and importance of group work practice because, group work is not merely conducting activities but this conducting of different social activities is the means to do group work. Let us now discuss the various components of group work in detail.

Formation of Groups

The students should know the norms or requirements of forming groups of the children/youth from their respective supervisors. The following norms should be considered:

(a) Number of group members,
(b) Age groups of the group members, and
(c) Size of group.

With this preparation and understanding the students should contact the agency supervisor and collect the names of the children/youth. These students should be called for the purpose. Technical difficulties like delay in getting the names of group members from the agencies, children not available for some time or other such difficulties may arise. Each student, as a group leader, should overcome such difficulties on his own as soon as possible. The required skills will have to be developed, otherwise they will remain dependent on the faculty for everything.

The children called for the purpose should be introduced first. Information regarding the programme, objectives, timetable, etc., should then be given to them in brief. The day, time and place of the programme should also be intimated. The group workers should always remember that their regularity and punctuality is very important because this will influence the personality of the group members. If the group workers (student leaders) are not available on any fieldwork day, they should inform the group members well in advance otherwise it may have a negative impact on the group members. It should be well understood that such communication is required to be given otherwise remaining absent without any intimation to the group members and the agency personnel would send wrong signals to the members. Also in doing so an indication is sent to the group members on the importance of such communication.

Induction of Group Members

Students or group workers should collect personal information of the members of the group for their knowledge and understanding in one or two visits in the beginning. The following format may be used for the purpose.

S. No.	*Name*	*Age*	*Education*	*Caste/ Religion*	*Hobbies*	*Habits*	*Interests*	*Prizes*

With this personal data the group workers or the trainee students should collect the family data of the group members for understanding the socio-economic and socio-cultural background for the purpose of group work process. The following format may be referred to for the purpose.

S. No.	*Name of the Family Member*	*Age*	*Education*	*Occupa- tion*	*Income*	*Caste*	*Problems*	*Comforts*

After collection of personal and family data of group members, the group workers or the students should interact with the group members and try to collect information about the problems of the members and their family members for identifying problematic cases for casework practice. Such members should be helped to solve their problems with the help of casework method. Study of the personal and family information assists the students in casework practice.

Conducting Sports Activities

Generally, it has been observed that children or group members always like to play games rather than involve themselves in any other activities or programmes. Considering this interest, the group workers should start their programmes with sports activities. The members should preferably be allowed to choose the game/s. However, the group workers should see whether the facilities required for playing a particular game are available. The trainee students should remember that from the social workers' point of view, the entire game activity revolves around their observing the attitudes of the participants. They must observe the actions, reactions, interests and participation levels of the participants. The entire observational process should include making necessary notes for further help in counselling and guidance. This observation should be followed up with suggestions to the members who are not participating and reacting properly towards the game or group. Such members should be helped to solve their problems with the help of casework method. These observations should be recorded in the dairies and journals and after providing necessary professional help the changes should be observed and noted. If the group worker or the students are not able to understand certain attitudes or have difficulty in assessment of certain behavioural patterns, discussions should be held with the agency and faculty supervisors. Necessary corrective action can then be initiated.

A brief report should be prepared and submitted later to the agency supervisors by the group workers along with their opinions and suggestions.

Conducting Sanskar Programmes

The group workers or the students should arrange for *sanskar* programmes to be conducted. These are programmes through which *sanskars* or cultural values can be imbibed in the children. Such programmes should be prepared/chalked out considering the age group and educational status of the group members. Generally children are interested in short stories, poems, songs and religious *shlokas* or *mantras.* While choosing stories and poems it should be taken into account that the stories or poems relate to a moral and also to the children first. The following are some stories, which can be narrated for the purpose:

(i) Story of the Honest Wood-Cutter: Truth Always Pays.
(ii) Story of Shravan Bal: Love and Respect for Parents.
(iii) Story of king Bruce of Scotland: Try and Try; Success is Sure.
(iv) Story of The Shepherd Boy: Never Tell Lies.
(v) Story of Haste is Waste: Think Before you Leap.
(vi) Story of Two Parrots: Impact of Environment.
(vii) Aesop's Fables, Stories from Panchatantra: Morals.

Students or group workers should select simple stories which can be enjoyed by children, while also conveying a message which could be learnt. Students should prepare the story-telling exercise well before presenting it to the group members. Even as they narrate the purposeful stories, the group members' responses, grasping, understanding should be observed carefully. After the story-telling programmes are completed, discussions should be held with group members to know and understand the internalisation of the morals/central ideas in their personalities. The impact of the stories should be examined whenever the group workers find time. They must also find out the individual group member's perception and the utility of the central theme for his personality development. The observations and the impact on the group members should be recorded in diaries and a brief report prepared for group work practice before being submitted to the agency supervisors for their use.

Similarly, group workers should select certain poems and songs that carry specific messages of learning. The selection of poems and songs should be done considering the age group, educational status and interest of the members of the group. The following poems/ songs can be referred to for teaching.

(i) Martin Luther King's *Hum honge kaamyaab* (original English version).
(ii) Dr. Iqbal's *Saare jahaanse achha Hindustan hamara.*
(iii) National Songs:
- Ravindranath Tagore's *Jana gana mana adhi nayaka jaya he*.
- Bankim Chandra Chatterjee's *Vande maataram sujalam sufalam malayaja seetalam*.

(iv) Patriotic and meaningful filmy songs.

Group workers should study the songs and prepare well for teaching the songs and poems. The group workers should observe the responses of the members and involve them in the teaching and learning processes, by which the group members will be able to internalise the central message of the poem or song. The teaching and its impact on the members should be examined after some time. A brief report should be prepared and submitted to the agency supervisors for their use and record.

The same is the case when the group workers teach certain phrases, which carry messages of learning. The procedure followed for the story-telling, teaching of poems and songs should be followed here also. The phrase and idioms mentioned below can be referred to for teaching.

(i) A chip of the old block: a worthy son of a worthy father.
(ii) Jack of all trades: a man who devotes himself to many occupations.
(iii) To be true to one's salt: to be faithful to one's employer.
(iv) To build castles in the air: to form visionary schemes.
(v) To carry the day: to win.
(vi) Black sheep: bad character.
(vii) Crocodile tears: pretended grief.
(viii) Wild goose chase: foolish adventure.
(ix) To break the ice: to begin to speak after a long awkward silence.
(x) To burn one's fingers: to cause grief.

Conducting Tests on General Studies

There exists competition in all fields today. Two inherent components of competition are winning and losing. To appreciate and enjoy a win and to take courage in a loss are two most important virtues. Children should be taught to face challenges. They have to be motivated and prepared for this. Not everyone can enter and succeed in this competitive field. There are many reasons due to which they lag behind. Considering these conditions or situations the group workers should prepare or chalk out certain programmes to motivate the group members to enter various competitions as well as to enhance their knowledge and develop their personalities. Different kinds of competitions should be conducted to help group members for the purpose.

(i) Essay competition,
(ii) Elocution competition,
(iii) Drawing competition,
(iv) Handwriting competition,
(v) Spelling competition, and
(vi) Vocabulary competition.

Such competitions will help the group members to prepare for and enhance their knowledge, and come out with hidden talents that they may possess. This will change the way they think and develop their outlook also. For this, the subject given to the group members for essay and elocution competitions should be important from the point of view of their personality development. Generally the subjects should pertain to the social aspects and/or national integration theme. The following subjects can be referred or used for the purpose.

(i) Old Customs
(ii) Popular Superstition
(iii) Travel as a part of Education
(iv) The best way of Spending Holidays
(v) Your Favourite Hobbies
(vi) The Forming of Habits
(vii) Fashions
(viii) How you hope to Continue your Education when you Leave School.
(ix) My Great Wish
(x) Good Manners
(xi) The Influence of Cinema
(xii) The Pleasure of Reading
(xiii) The Use and Abuse of Leisure
(xiv) My Country

(xv) National Symbols and Festivals
(xvi) National Integration
(xvii) Life Histories of National Leaders
(xviii) Some incidents from the Life of National Leaders
(xix) Small Speeches
(xx) Should Boys learn to Cook.

Celebrating National Festivals

Through group work practices the young generation should be made aware of the significance of national and religious festivals. To create awareness among them it is necessary to teach the background and messages given through the national and religious festivals. The proper meaning and understanding is to be brought out before the young generation. The group workers should study the national and religious festivals well and celebrate the festivals with group members and explain to them the central reasons as to why the festivals are being celebrated. They should be asked to write about them and also to deliver a lecture on the day of the celebration. After sometime their perception and internalisation of these may be studied. The group workers should remember that there are no hard and fast rules to be followed regarding any timetable or schedule in celebrating national holidays and festivals. The national festivals can be celebrated on the same day or any other day. The following national festival holidays can be celebrated with the group members:

(i) Independence Day
(ii) Republic Day
(iii) Dusshera
(iv) Diwali
(v) Raksha Bandhan
(vi) Makar Sankaranti
(vii) Christmas
(viii) New Year
(ix) Ramzan Id
(x) Bakrid
(xi) Onam and other important festivals

Arranging and Celebrating Anniversaries of Great Personalities

Great personalities are always remembered for their greatness. The young generation of today may not be aware of their contribution to society. So, the group workers should arrange programmes for celebration of the anniversaries of great persons. It is necessary that the group workers should study the contributions of such persons well and teach the group members about their devotion, dedication, sacrifices, etc. The group members should be asked to prepare essays and lectures, and they should be given opportunities to present and exercise it in a group. This will help them to inculcate the great thoughts of these men into their personalities. Influencing the members by these depends on the efforts, techniques and methods of group workers. The group workers also develop their own personalities in the course of all these efforts. As in the other activities, here also it is necessary to study the impact of celebration of important leaders' birth and death anniversaries on the group members. Again it is suggested that notes be maintained. The group workers can refer to the following list for celebration of birth and death anniversaries of

(i) Mahatma Gandhi,
(ii) Subhash Chandra Bose,
(iii) Pandit Jawaharlal Nehru,
(iv) Veer Sawarkar,
(v) Vinoba Bhave,
(vi) Jaiprakash Narayan,
(vii) Dr. Babasaheb Ambedkar,
(viii) Lal Bahadhur Shastri,
(ix) Indira Gandhi and Rajiv Gandhi, and
(x) Gulzarilal Nanda.

Organisation of Cultural Programmes

Organising cultural programmes and excursions are of vital importance for the development of the personalities of the children. Their interest in such activities is very keen. Cultural programmes should be prepared considering the interest of the group members. A time schedule can also be prepared in consultation with the agency and faculty supervisors. The significance of the selected cultural programmes should be explained in detail and then the activities be conducted. Like cultural programmes the children always take interest in the outings. Through purposeful recreations and exchange of ideas in the group, the group workers should observe the response, behaviours, actions and reactions and note these down for guidance and counselling services. The group workers also learn many things while teaching or practising group work theory.

Arranging a Parents Meet

It is necessary to interact with the parents of the group members to bring out the weaknesses, strengths and needs of the children for their interventions at the proper time to take care and develop the personalities of the children. The group workers should bring to the notice of the parents, the observations of group members for the purpose of initiating corrective actions as may be required and to create awareness in the parents about the behaviours and attitudes of the children. Generally, parents are emotional and they carry ideas in their minds that their children are allright and are doing well in the schools. It may be a little difficult at first, but once they are convinced they realise their fault. At times, it is too late and they repent for their own negligence. Such professional interactions may help them to correct the shortcomings in time. The group workers should give necessary guidance and counselling to the parents. A brief report of this activity should be prepared and submitted to the agency supervisors and the same should be recorded in the journals of the group workers for evaluation.

Guidance and Counselling

The group workers should observe and collect information regarding the interests, hobbies, needs and shortcomings of the group members and guide or counsel them about the same. Most of the times these are neglected. The group workers should prepare a brief report and submit it to the agency supervisors along with recommendations and also bring it to the notice of the children members. The guidance and counselling services help the group members to learn or practice proper things and it also assist the group workers to learn the guidance and counselling process practically.

Conducting Exit Interviews

It is essential to conduct interviews of the group members to understand the changes in their approaches, attitudes and behaviour that have taken place as a result of the group work programmes. Their opinions and suggestions must be sought regarding the activities conducted during the academic year. On the basis of their interviews a brief report should be prepared and submitted to the agency supervisors. A record of this must also be kept in the journal.

Send-off Programme

A common programme should be organised in the agency with the group members being allowed to share their experiences about the group work programmes and their learning from these programmes. Similarly, the group workers should also express their views. Photographs of the group could be taken for remembrance.

Follow-up Programme

At the end of the academic year the social work students stop going to the group work agencies and start preparing for their annual examinations. Due to this, they do not practise the follow-up programmes, which are very essential in social work profession. Despite genuine difficulties follow-up programmes can also be practised as under:

(i) The same group can be attached to the next batch of social work students of the new academic year for follow-up practices and the group work process can be continued.

(ii) The group worker should be asked to collect the addresses of the group members, so that they can be personally contacted during the next academic year for the follow-up programme. Faculty supervisors should take personal interest in encouraging the follow-up programmes. However, this depends on the practice in each school.

Report on Fieldwork Seminar

(i) Name of the student :

(ii) Name of the school :

(iii) Batch number :

(iv) Name of the faculty :

(v) The seminar paper written by the student on group :

(vi) Participation of the student in the seminar and questions raised for discussion :

(vii) Supported the views/answers of colleagues or explained answers properly in the seminar :

(viii) Exchange of ideas and opinions recorded suggestions, if any

(ix) Assisted in organising the seminar : :

(x) Special contribution of the student in the seminar, if any :

(xi) Use of guidance of the supervisor for participation and discussion :

(xii) Observation in the seminar, if any :

Remarks:

Signature (Faculty Supervisor) Signature (Student)

Group Work Recordings

The group work students should record the programmes and the responses of the group members in the group work diaries, journals and reports. This recording is necessary for the following purposes:

(i) Evaluation of the performance of the group workers in examinations,

(ii) As proof of participation of the group members,

(iii) To identify changes in their approaches and attitudes,

(iv) For evaluation of use of the group work practices for solutions to problems of individuals through group work,

(v) For maintaining records in the agencies, and

(vi) For developing a library of literature on social work.

Systematic recording seems to be a difficult task specially for the rural students. Therefore, some model writings are given here for reference and learning.

Group Work Diary

The group worker or the trained students should be clear about the objectives or purposes of writing diaries. The recordings in group work diaries should be done according to the activities and observations of the responses of the group members. It should be brief and to the point. However, the observation about responses should invariably be mentioned because it is very difficult to remember every little detail and the group worker may forget important observations while writing journals and dealing with group members in future. Model write-ups may be referred to.

Model 1

Visit No.:
Day:
Date:

The members were interested in making some paper articles. So they were allowed to make the articles. By discussing and exchanging ideas with everyone, the group members made articles like kites, dolls, vehicles, animals, birds, etc. Their feelings, ideas and cooperation made them learn many things. They developed team spirit and unity, which helped them establish healthy relationships and group feelings.

Signature	Signature	Signature
(Agency Supervisor)	(Faculty Supervisor)	(Student)

Model 2

Visit No.:
Day:
Date:

Today the group members were interested in listening to stories from the group workers, so a short story of The Wood-cutter was told for their entertainment and also to communicate a message of truth and its significance.

Everyone should observe truth in the life. The group members were pleased to learn the message given through the story.

Signature	Signature	Signature
(Agency Supervisor)	(Faculty Supervisor)	(Student)

Model 3

Visit No.:
Day:
Date:

For a change the group members wished to discuss The topic, picnic. Everyone was speaking about it except one persons, who was not expressing his opinion or interest at all. This was pointed out to the group. To learn the reason for his silence he was called away from the place for maintaining confidentiality. He related his problems. To solve his problem it was found necessary to counsel him. After this the date for a picnic was also fixed up.

Signature	Signature	Signature
(Agency Supervisor)	(Faculty Supervisor)	(Student)

Model 4

Visit No.:
Day:
Date:

Today the group members were interested in learning the work of Mahatma Gandhi regarding the scavenger community. So a lecture was delivered on his work and contribution in the field. The group members also asked questions and discussed in detail and decided to write an essay on this topic.

Signature	Signature	Signature
(Agency Supervisor)	(Faculty Supervisor)	(Student)

Group Work Journal

The group work journal should be written in detail based on the notes in the diaries. The notes should be elaborated and written in the journals from a practical point of view. The practical aspects should be emphasised with illustrations, diagrams, graphs, etc. Generally students of social work in the suburbs are found writing journals as they would write diaries, in which, irrelevant details are included like, visited the agency, met the supervisor and discussed about group work, etc. Specific activities, their practice, response of the group members and observations, etc., ought to be mentioned. To help such students prepare better journals, a few model journal writings are shown below for reference:

Examples of Group Work Journals

1

Visit No.:
Day:
Date:

Group Formation

Being a group work leader the group worker contacted the headmaster of the school allotted to him. The headmaster spared 11 children of the eighth standard as per the decision taken during the earlier visit on request of our school/school of social work. The 11 children also showed interest in involving themselves. Their acceptance was very important from the professional social worker's point of view. Their interest and acceptance encouraged the group worker to form this group. After this he called all the selected children to the ground and elaborated the purpose and importance of fieldwork, group unity, its benefits, etc. All the children happily expressed their willingness to follow all the instructions, rules and regulations of the programme and the directions given to them from time to time. Their commitment, enthusiastic participation and cooperation was appreciated and welcomed. For identification a name was to be given to the group. The principle of democracy was followed and the students themselves were asked to suggest a name. According to the majority of the members of the group the name "Jagruti" was finally agreed upon. Further information of the group was collected in the following format:

S. No.	*Name*	*Father's Name*	*Surname*	*Age*	*Class*

The group worker then met the headmaster and briefed him about the entire session with the students. He also conveyed the enthusiasm and eagerness shown by the students in participating in a programme of this kind. The headmaster was very pleased to note these details and wished to know more about group work practice. The group worker felt elated and happy as he now had an opportunity of informing the headmaster, how different this practice was from normal sports activities and other group activities like that of NSS.

2

Visit No.:
Day:
Date:

Personal Data

After forming the groups the group members assembled on the school ground according to the timetable. They were eager to know about the programmes but before preparing the programmes it was necessary to collect the personal and family data of the group members. So the group worker conducted interviews to collect the necessary information as under:

(i) Name of the member :
(ii) Age :
(iii) Sex :
(iv) Caste :
(v) Class :
(vi) Mother tongue :
(vii) Hobbies :
(viii) Habits :
(ix) Likes and dislikes :

(x) Interest :
(xi) Performance in the school :
(xii) Prizes :
(xiii) General physical appearance :
(xiv) Father's name and age :
(xv) Mother's name and age :
(xvi) Names of other family members and age :
(xvii) Educational background of family members :
(xviii) Occupation :
(xix) Income and expenditure :

The data of one of the group members was studied. It is concluded from his family background that it is a joint family. He has well-adjusted attitudes, approaches, likes and dislikes, interests, etc., because he is used to the joint family system which has many members of different types. It is found that he is interested in students because of the ideal members of his family. With this background information the group worker met his teacher to know about him. The teacher revealed that the boy was very sharp in studies. The group worker's interest is to study the child and to guide and motivate him for further development.

Signature (Agency Supervisor)	Signature (Faculty Supervisor)	Signature (Student)

3

Visit No.:
Day:
Date:

Game of Lagori

The personal data of all the members were collected with the help of interview method and their background was studied carefully to prepare programmes considering their interest, zeal, need and demand. In the beginning, the group members expressed their feelings that they wished to play the game of *lagori*. Accordingly, *lagori* was played. The group members had brought their own ball. The group worker asked them to make two groups, i.e., Group A and Group B and two members were made the group leaders. The groups were as follows:

A Team		*B Team*	
S. No.	*Name*	*S. No.*	*Name*

The group members brought five flat circular pieces of stone. These were then stacked one over the other to make a *lagori.* Twenty minutes were allotted to each team to play this game. As per the rules, one team has to throw the ball and the other team has to catch it to make them out. There was a toss to decide who would begin the game. Team A called heads and won the toss. So, Team A started the game. Team A started throwing the ball and Team B tried catching it to get the players out. However, after five minutes the group worker found that the members were not aware of certain rules. So the game was stopped for a while and the rules of the game were explained clearly as under:

Rules of Lagori

- There should be two teams.
- There should be a distance of at least five feet between the *lagori* and the line from which the ball would be thrown.
- There are only three chances to throw the ball and hit the lagori.
- The member who falls down on the *lagori* on his own is given out.
- The fielding party should not hide the ball.

After explanation of the rules the game started again. Due to interest of the members the game also become interesting. Team A scored two points and Team B one. And so Team A won the game. Members of Team A danced with joy and started teasing the other team members who were getting irritated. Here the group worker intervened and gently pointed out that discipline should be maintained. Secondly, in any game there will be winners and losers. There should be a spirit of sportsmanship. Some other day, perhaps, the winning team may lose. All members resumed their good behaviour after that.

Observation

All the 12 members played the game with interest and zeal. However, the performance of all the members was not the same. Some members were found active and others not so. One child was found to be lonely even while playing. He was playing the game without enthusiastic involvement. The group worker tried to make him play twice, but on both occassions when he diverted his attention to others, the boy would become aloof. After the game the group worker called him separately and inquired about his disinterest in the game. It was felt that the boy had some problem so the group worker decided to do casework practice and help him solve his problem on his own.

Role of the Leader

The group worker explained the rules to the members and showed them how to play the game of *lagori* and the group members also followed and played the game. When Team A won, the group worker appreciated and congratulated them for their victory and consoled Team B. The group worker then explained to them where they had failed and wished them good luck the next time. This encouragement motivated them and helped to enhance their confidence.

Think and Do

"Observe the actions and reactions of the members of different groups in which you live, i.e., family, friends circle and the like, and assist the needy to develop their personalities."

Chapter 6

Work with Community

"Training in community settings helps students learn social work practice with an integrated approach."

Fieldwork training in community organisations is an old method of training. The schools of social work in India introduced it only in the 1960s and 1980s. Yet, the schools in moffussil area have neglected it till today. It must be noted that even those schools that practice this method have not prepared any specific practical syllabi based on theory. In spite of this, students are placed in community settings, who then practice under the guidance and supervision of the faculty supervisors and somehow try and complete their training. The experts in this line have developed certain models of community organisation but the rural students do not understand them. Therefore, the author has made an attempt to discuss the procedure, methods and practices to be followed in the community settings on the basis of his personal experiences and observations.

Need for Placement in Community Settings

Placement of the students in community settings is the need of the hour. It enables the schools to impart training in social work education with an integrated fieldwork approach on the basis of the needs of the community. This is very important because the students themselves are involved in framing the policies as well as implementing them. Such opportunities are not given to students when they are placed in agency settings. Moreover, professional welfare services can be rendered to the needy in the selected community, which would help the schools not only to provide an open, unbinding opportunity to students to work freely, but also at the same time earn goodwill, recognition and name in society. Additionally it has been seen that there are voluntary organisations working in the areas who attempt to identify the needs of these areas and try to satisfy them. Most often, though these organisations identify the needs they don't succeed in solving them because their reach and resources are restricted. Schools of social work generally have necessary knowledge regarding the ways of identifying and reaching the sources of help. Thus communities would also benefit a lot through such placements.

Objectives of Training in Community Organisation

The objectives of fieldwork training in community organisation are as under:

- To provide an opportunity to the students of first year to practise all methods of social work, i.e., fieldwork, casework, group work, community organisation, social welfare administration, social work research and social action with an integrated approach.
- To enable the students to understand the lives of people living in communities, their ways of thinking, attitudes, approaches, outlooks, general and specific problems faced by them, their needs, etc.
- To help the students learn the art of framing policies and to work independently in the field under the guidance and control of the faculty supervisors.
- To assist the students in learning the art of interaction with people, relating to their needs and problems.
- To provide an opportunity for the students to deal with individuals in groups and communities.
- To provide an opportunity to the students to learn different kinds of problems and cases.
- To enable the students to set up independent agencies for fieldwork training where community development projects can be implemented with or without aid from the government.
- To appoint MSWs in Community Development Projects on a regular monthly stipend or salary to guide the trainee students with interest, zeal and a professional approach.

- To bypass any non co-operating social agency, as also untrained and disinterested agency supervisors.
- To encourage the students to set up voluntary organisations in the selected communities in urban as well as rural areas for self-employment and also to develop professional services needed in the community.

Methods and Procedure of Self-Study

The students must study the above objectives and the following methods carefully. Only then can they fulfil the demands of the community. The following methods of fieldwork training could be followed:

- Theoretical preparation before proceeding to the community.
- Scientific analysis of the theory.
- Professional discussions with the faculty supervisors.
- Scientific observation of the community.
- Professional interaction with people, experts, leaders and the concerned grassroots level workers.
- Participation in the activities of the organisations existing in the community.
- Working in the community and practising social work.

Community organisation has its own theory, philosophy and principles. Without preparing the theoretical background the students will not be able to carry out their practicals. Therefore, they should bear in mind that theory should be prepared thoroughly to understand the working of the community organisation. After that they should analyse the critical aspects pointed out in the theory. A comparative study of theory and the actual realities with the help of general reading and common sense should be done. This helps the students understand the basics of community organisation. With this basic preparation they can discuss with their faculty supervisors. Professional discussions with experts always add to basic knowledge, and will help them in gaining conceptual clarity. This conceptual clarity paves the way for learning practical aspects with ease. Now, students should move around in the community and observe the lives of people living there and interact with them. This will enhance their practical knowledge and help them in shaping their views. After the sociological field study the students should begin work in the community with the help of social work techniques studied.

Procedure of Fieldwork

Scientific practice in social work settings have not been developed in the schools of social work in moffussil areas of our country. There is no manual or procedure of work that could be followed. However, training is being imparted through verbal guidance by the faculty supervisors and students normally are not able to carry out the correct form of fieldwork in communities. Considering this practical difficulty the procedure of fieldwork is discussed here in detail. The following general guidelines will enable them to select the proper community for the purpose of fieldwork-training-cum-community-development:

- The community should be physically accessible to both schools and students.
- It should be safe for girl students.
- Necessary basic facilities should be available.
- The community should have the need for social welfare services, identified either by professional social workers or the schools of social work.
- People living in the community should show interest, zeal and enthusiasm in the service, they want to be rendered by the schools.
- People living in the community should be ready to mobilise local resources for their own development.
- They should communicate freely with the schools regarding their needs.

Selection of Community

A suitable community should be selected on the basis of the general guidelines and information available in the schools. This selection should be based on the needs of the community and should be taken up with a view to rendering services to the needy and the community at large. A team of faculty members along with students should pay a visit to the community to have an overview of the geographical area of the community, so as to judge its suitability. After that the community should be finally selected for training and development.

Data Regarding General Background

Students should visit the selected community on the fieldwork days fixed by the schools. To begin with, the entire team of fieldwork students should mingle and interact with group leaders or people of stature in the community, to understand the sociological background of different castes and religious groups. Such information is vital for planning further programmes. The information sheet devised for the purpose of collecting the information could be used for the record and proper induction.

Information Sheet of the Community

(i)	Name	:	
(ii)	Type of community	:	(Rural/Urban/Suburban / Slum)
(iii)	Location	:	
(iv)	Total population	:	(Male/Female)
(v)	Number of the households	:	
(vi)	Main sources of income	:	
(vii)	Number of social organisation	:	
(viii)	Main language of the community	:	
(ix)	Major problems and needs	:	
(x)	Sanitary conditions	:	(Good/Average/Bad)
(xi)	Major area of fieldwork project	:	
(xii)	Title of the fieldwork project	:	
(xiii)	Duration of the project	:	
(xiv)	Name/s of the fieldwork trainee/s	:	
(xv)	Name of the faculty supervisors	:	
(xvi)	Name of the school of social work	:	
(xvii)	Batch number	:	

Social Survey

The information regarding general background of the community will help the students to understand the situation the community is presently in. However, it is necessary to study the socio-economic, socio-cultural and socio-political background of the people for further process. For this, a small survey should be conducted under the guidance of the faculty supervisors. The primary data collected through the empirical survey should be analysed and a simple project report prepared for reference and planning of the programmes and activities, and their execution. This would provide to the students their first opportunity in learning how to start work on scientific lines in any community.

Identifying the Needs of the People

Theoretical preparation, a cursory survey and observation of the community will help the students to understand the essence of the community and based on that they can establish purposeful relations. Once this rapport is established, the students should interact with as many people as possible to find out their actual needs, interests, mental preparation or readiness to mobilise resources, etc. Professional interactions with the community leaders will help them identify the real needs. These needs should be recorded for reference and perusal whenever needed. The following format devised for the purpose may be used:

Priority Base Felt Needs

S. No.	*Felt Needs*	*Duration of the Need*	*Who would be the Beneficiaries*	*What would be the Cost*	*What would be the Cost Benefit*	*Possible Resources Available*

Meeting with the Leaders

The community leaders may be working on different lines or on different issues of the community under different political philosophies but it is necessary to call a meeting of such leaders on a common platform for achieving the goal. This may be possible only when sufficient and reliable data are collected regarding the working of the leaders. The data must then be studied thoroughly, otherwise it will be impossible to convince them. The data pertaining to the leaders irrespective of caste, colour, creed and political affiliations could be collected in the following format.

Particulars of Local Leaders

S. No.	*Name and Address*	*Whether Politician/ Social Worker/ Youth Leader*	*The Nature of Services/ Assistance that the Community could Expect from them*

The leaders are to be dealt with carefully. A minor mistake or negligence on the part of the students could create a major problem, which may become a hurdle in the social work training-cum- practice process. Therefore, these personalities, most of them with inflated egos, are to be handled skillfully. They should be convinced to attend a meeting meant for the purpose of welfare of the community at large. Students could face a few problems, but their constant efforts, integrity and belief in social work philosophy will help them to overcome these. The meeting should be conducted systematically and the problems and urgent needs of the community should be discussed on a common platform in such a way that a common decision is arrived at, even when dealing with leaders having varied approaches. While such meetings pave the way to progress, they also increase the communication skills and administrative qualities of the students.

Professional Individual Help

From social interactions, survey analyses, meetings, general discussions and observations in the community it will be possible for the students to collect information regarding the individual needs and problems of the people. After individual cases have been identified, they should be guided and counselled to help themselves and casework should be practised under the guidance of faculty supervisors. This being an open community the students will find freedom to use their skills, methods and procedures to deal with the individuals. There are no restrictions on the students unlike in voluntary organisations. They can handle the cases right from the preparation of case sheets to evaluation reports. This is how casework training can be imparted and professional services rendered in the community.

Professional Group Help

Man is called a social animal because he spends most of his time in groups. There are different kinds of groups, i.e., friends circle, youth organisations, schools and the like. Trainee students should contact such groups for the sake of their all-round development. They may face problems in the beginning but their constant efforts, art, skills of dealing with human beings will see them through. Once the groups are formed the trainee students should start practising group work for their all-round development and individual cases should also be identified from the groups for casework practice. Group work practice in the community can be done systematically without any pressure, restrictions or policies such as in the agencies. Students can frame their own polices and follow the methods and procedures devised by them independently, but, consultation with the faculty supervisors is mandatory.

Community Development

Any social organisation operating in the community should be visited and studied to understand its nature, structure, condition and position. Such information will be needed to plan developmental programmes. The data may be collected in the following format devised for the purpose.

Particulars of Social Organisations in the Community

S. No.	*Name and Address*	*Nature of Service*	*Type of Beneficiaries*	*In Operation Since*

The students will get an idea regarding the working of social organisations from the data. They should plan out the programmes and encourage more people to set up different types of organisations like *Tarun Mandals* (youth associations), *Mahila Mandals* (women's organisations), *Bhajan Mandals* and different other kinds of agencies. Necessary guidelines should be given to the people, on registration, preparation of documents, etc. Professional help should be provided to both old and newly setup organisations to carry out the functions. Various programmes should be devised and implemented scientifically. However, the trainee students should have knowledge regarding the funding agencies and practice, necessary coordination, and administrative capabilities for getting help for the community.

Besides providing guidelines and proper coordination in the social agencies, either set up earlier or set up through the efforts of the students, the following projects should be implemented for training-cum-development:

- Self-employment or income-generating projects for economic development.
- School social work projects to provide solutions to, and prevention of problems of the students.
- Child care projects for preventive and remedial services.
- Health and family welfare projects for preventive and curative services, and constructive work for improving the quality of the life.
- Youth welfare projects to care for vagabonds and delinquents.
- Community care projects for activating the community people to keep their community clean through constructive efforts.
- Community action project for creating awareness among the people towards their needs, problems, rights and duties.
- Professional counselling service projects for rendering counselling services for day-to-day problems which, otherwise lead to family disorganisation.
- Vocational guidance projects for providing information to the people pertaining to employment and career development.
- Women welfare projects to create awareness among women against their exploitation, and to fight for their rights and responsibilities.

- Senior citizens welfare projects for providing required facilities, i.e., recreation and utilisation of their experience for the community.
- Counselling projects for alcoholics.

Forming Public Opinion

Programmes like guidance, counselling, helping individuals, groups and community at large should be continued, but along with these the trainee students should try to solve certain specific social problems of the people with the help of social action method. For this, public opinion must be formed against evil consequences of the problems. Public opinion can be formed with the help of different methods like exhibition of posters, organising street plays, rallies, slogans, discussions, lectures, publishing articles, etc. This process will assist the students to understand the social action method practically. They also contribute to eradication of certain social problems. This is how fieldwork training can be imparted to the students of social work education in community settings. The experiment conducted by the author could be studied as an example of case study, answers could be found to the questions raised in the process and an effort to overcome them, while performing similar work could be made.

Experiment of Fieldwork Training in Open Community Setting

TAPASWEE

TAPASWEE is an association of trained and professional social workers, started in March 1989. Our main aim is to organise a team of professional social workers, to bring improvement in the quality and quantity of services rendered by them and to establish demonstrative models evolved for the scientific and planned practice of social work.

In order to bring this objective into practice TAPASWEE started working in Sushil Nagar and Kamala Nagar community from March 1989. We do not claim this action programme to be an adoption of a community because our professional philosophy is “Community development through people in the community”. Our intervention in the community development process is to create awareness among them and provide the required expertise whenever possible.

How it Began

TAPASWEE activists, along with practitioners working in the field, visited three different communities and made attempts to study the feasibility of social work practice in a community. The following points were considered in selecting the said community:

(a) Practice of professional social work and use of available resources;
(b) Awareness among the people regarding professional social work;
(c) Local leadership and participation of people in community development programmes; and
(d) Socio-cultural conditions of the people in the community.

The simple reason for selecting the Sushil Nagar and Kamala Nagar community was that it was comparatively untouched from the professional social work point of view. It may be argued that more scientific and systematic efforts could have been made for selecting a better community. But TAPASWEE activists, being practitioners in the field, used their experiential discretion. Followed by the general consensus on selecting the community, a systematic survey was conducted. Initially 200 families, representative in character, were considered for the study. As in the case of other urban communities, this group too had multidimensional problems and corresponding needs. It was felt that working on all levels at a time would not be possible due to limitations on the number of activists. So TAPASWEE decided to concentrate initially only on health and education of the people.

Agency for Fieldwork Training

A detailed report analysing the needs and areas of intervention by professional social workers was prepared and discussed by the activists of TAPASWEE. This was submitted to the Director, Department of Social Work, Walchand School, Solapur, requesting for placement of MSW students as Fieldwork Trainees. Our request was accepted and ten students were placed as trainees from July 1989. Due to the non-availability of curriculum for fieldwork training in an open community setting, TAPASWEE started in its own way with a strong determination of evolving a need-based curriculum.

Agency Supervision

TAPASWEE had no full time staff members. Sunita Tarapure and Manjiri Deshpande, the Directors of TAPASWEE, came forward to shoulder the responsibility of supervision of the student trainees. They were assigned this job since they had been involved in this action project since its inception. They had to learn along with the learners because they had not had any instructional training themselves in agency supervision. This approach proved better and helped the students exchange their views more freely. Of course, the other formalities in accordance with the norms laid down by the Shivaji University were strictly followed.

Fieldwork Training

In the beginning, students were acclimatised to community living and asked to establish a functional relationship within the community by door-to-door visits and meaningful interaction with the people. In order to develop a demonstrative model for fieldwork training, an integrated approach was considered.

Integrated Fieldwork Training: Our Style

Social work practice in community health presupposes an understanding and study of macro and micro level factors affecting the individual's and society's interpretation of health and ill health (beliefs, prejudices, resistance, stigma, etc.) To understand this better, the students were asked to make a systematic study by following the methods of social work research. It may not be a full-fledged scientific study but this helped students to get a conceptual understanding of the situation.

With this background the students started planning programmes in community health, both on preventive and curative levels. They concentrated on existing health care delivery systems. They were also taught to make use of the available resources in the field. This exercise gave them a practical understanding of social welfare administration. When the students with planned functional relationship began to socialise with the people in the community, they came across a variety of problems. These problems were discussed among the students in the presence of the agency and faculty supervisors, and cases were identified to be handled by the students for social casework. Local leaders also helped in bringing more cases and discussing participatory treatment process. Students learnt to handle a variety of cases independently. To mention a few, Kamala, a deserted women with a child, needing help in a legal action against her 22-year-old husband, Rajendra, who became a paraplegic through an accident while doing his duty; Gopal, a blind boy wanting admission in a blind school; Seema, a school dropout; Surendra, a physically handicapped boy; and many other such cases.

Group formation was difficult for the students in the open community setting. Unfortunately there was no classroom teaching for students on this. So TAPASWEE organised a workshop, to teach group therapy and other related concepts. Subsequently, students started working with youth, women and children in the community. They formed groups with their own set of criteria and according to their own understanding of the situation. They felt that tenth class students had the need for guidance, and hence they formed a group for poor and needy students, and started "guidance classes" with the help of interested local school teachers. The class activity gave the students a new opening and simultaneously the tenth class students also started coming forward with suggestions for other activities besides guidance. The entire group realised their potential and student trainees were now fully confident of forming a group of the youth in the community. This exercise was allowed strictly according to principles and philosophies of group work.

The people in the community and active leadership gained confidence about their roles and contributions to community development programmes. They now started coming forward with suggestions regarding multi-purpose activities, which gave us a sense of real community organisation with people's participation. Slowly however, the community started expecting the students and TAPASWEE to lead social action on other issues like employment, health and sanitary systems, etc., and the students, having a very limited role, found it difficult to organise such activities.

TAPASWEE was at the crossroads, not because of our limitations but due to the limitations of fieldwork training system in social work education. This experience brought a very valid question before us. Since the student trainees are placed for a limited period only, what level should they be allowed to interview up to in an open community setting. As in this case, similar experimental probing efforts could bring many a limitations before us. These would certainly give rise to academic doubts and theoretical problems, the answers to which are still needed.

Fieldwork Guidance

To understand the core of practical work the students should meet their faculty supervisors on every fieldwork day for individual and group conferences. They should not be under the assumption that everything is understood or everything is available in books. Even richly experienced persons may be confused about certain complicated problems of people. Moreover, individual and group conferences increase communication skills, understanding and practical knowledge.

Government Schemes

The central and state governments (Ministry of Rural and Urban Development) have devised certain schemes of rural and urban development which are normally implemented through non-governmental organisations for the welfare of the people. The students should study these schemes, their nature, structure, funding, programmes, objectives, goals, etc. This information will not only be useful to guide people to set up their organisations to implement government projects and schemes but will also help the students to set up their own organisations, to create their own employment and to render service. Moreover, the students will obtain sound knowledge of their own field. Besides these governmental schemes, there are some foreign and private funding agencies, in the country who provide different projects to NGOs. These funding agencies and their projects should also be studied as a part of fieldwork training.

Send-off Programme

At the end of the year the students placed in a community setting should organise a send-off programme in the community to thank all the concerned persons for extending their cooperation. The addresses of the local leaders should be collected for communication in future.

Annual Fieldwork Seminar

After the send-off programmes in the communities, students should organise a fieldwork seminar to exchange their ideas and share the experiences gained in the process of fieldwork training or community development work. Professional experts may be invited to the seminar to assess their strengths and weakness. The guidance of the faculty supervisors may be sought to organise the seminar. Reports should be submitted to the fieldwork coordinator for record and evaluation. The model format devised for the purpose may be referred.

Report of Annual Fieldwork Seminar

1. Name of the student :
2. Name of the school :
3. Batch number :
4. Name of professor-in-charge :
5. Gist of the paper written by the student on community organisation and integrated fieldwork training for presentation in the seminar :
6. Participation in the conference/seminar and the questions raised for discussion :
7. Supported the answers of colleagues or explained answers clearly in the seminar :
8. Exchange of ideas and opinions and recording suggestions, if any :

9. Assisted in organising the conference and seminar on community organisation :
10. Special contribution of the student in seminar if any :
11. Observations of the students in seminar and practical gains :
12. Opinions and suggestions of the student :

Remarks:

Signature (Faculty) Signature (Student)

Self-Evaluation

After the seminar, students should submit their self-evaluation reports to the coordinator in the format prescribed for the purpose. The evaluation should be done honestly. They should not bother about their marks and rank because ultimately performance and knowledge are more important. The following model evaluation sheet devised for the purpose may be referred.

Model Self-Evaluation Format

1. Name of the student :
2. Name of the school :
3. Batch number :
4. Name of the faculty supervisor :
5. No. of visits paid during the year :
6. No. of cases identified and dealt with and individual performance :
7. Nature of group activities conducted during the year and individual performance :

8. No. of programmes organised for community organisation and individual performance :
9. No. of surveys conducted during the year and individual performance :
10. Methods used for formation of people against social problems and individual performance :
11. Participation and special interest of the student in community :
12. Observations and actual work done in the community and practical experiences gained for social work practice :
13. Nature of practical work experience gained through the fieldwork :
14. Opinion of the student regarding integrated fieldwork training :
15. Total hours worked in the community, individual performance and expectation of marks :

Remarks:

Signature (Faculty)	Signature (Student)

Recording Diary

Students of social work from the rural areas face problems in writing diaries. They mention visit numbers, time, meeting the supervisor and the concerned people, etc. These formalities should be avoided and diaries should be written in brief about the work done by the trainee students. The following model can be referred to:

Sample Diary of Community Work

1

Visit No.:
Day:
Date:

To identify the needs of the people in the selected community, my co-fieldworkers and I discussed with the community leaders at length and drew inferences that employment or work for women for supporting their families is their basic need. However, to gather information in detail, it has been decided to have an interaction with women directly next week.

Signature	Signature	Signature
(Agency Supervisor)	(Faculty Supervisor)	(Student)

2

Visit No.:
Day:
Date:

As decided last week my co-fieldworkers and I discussed with women living in the community and confirmed that employment was their primary need. In order to prepare a plan of action to find solutions, we discussed among ourselves and decided to talk it over with our faculty supervisors also the next week.

Signature	Signature	Signature
(Agency Supervisor)	(Faculty Supervisor)	(Student)

3

Visit No.:
Day:
Date:

According to our decision we discussed with our faculty

supervisors and called a meeting of the concerned people for a detailed discussion, to get their opinions and suggestions and take a democratic decision. The date, time and place were fixed and it was decided to communicate the decision to the people. For that an agenda was also prepared.

Signature (Agency Supervisor)	Signature (Faculty Supervisor)	Signature (Student)

4

Visit No.:
Day:
Date:

We went well in time to attend the meeting organised by us. The youth living in the community came early to help us. All the leaders, males and females attended the meeting. There was enthusiastic response from the people to our meeting. Our faculty supervisors addressed the meeting. Most of the members participated and a small ink production project was decided to be set up in the community.

Signature (Agency Supervisor)	Signature (Faculty Supervisor)	Signature (Student)

5

Visit No.:
Day:
Date:

According to the decisions taken in the last meeting with the community people, we decided to visit the office of the Industrial Development Corporation to find more about the proposed project and procedure for getting the facilities.

Signature (Agency Supervisor)	Signature (Faculty Supervisor)	Signature (Student)

Model of Journal Writing

Visit No.:
Day:
Date:

Introduction

Our school has placed me and four of my classmates in Kamala Nagar and Sushil Nagar slums in Solapur for fieldwork training in community setting. The faculty supervisor explained to us that he would be functioning as a faculty as well as agency supervisor for theory and practical guidance. We were very happy that we were placed in a community setting, because it enabled us to learn all the methods of social work practically. Moreover, it is possible to work with people directly. It is just like on-the-job training where real practical knowledge is gained. The community area was quite unknown but with a brief introduction and three observation rounds, we felt well acquainted with it.

Local Leaders

The actual work began with the introduction programme. The local leaders, irrespective of caste, colour and political affiliations were contacted. We then discussed the community structure, facilities, problems and difficulties to find out the needs of the people. From these talks with the leaders, a conclusion was drawn that women were in need of jobs to support their families because majority of the population was from the labour and lower middle class. This was the felt need of the community. However, we had no solutions for satisfying this need, as no one including the leaders, had any ideas. An attempt had earlier been made by some, but they could not do much. The main reasons for this inability was lack of a proper and healthy leadership.

Social Survey

On the basis of this general discussion we decided to do an interactional survey in the community. The students conducted a door-to-door survey. In this interactional survey also it was noticed that women were in need of some job or work. They were not able to do anything because they were illiterate due to which they were unable to unite themselves or to think of organising themselves. They wanted somebody to take the initiative in this regard.

Conclusion

It was concluded that the womenfolk were badly in need of jobs; they had thought of it earlier and expected someone to help. This general oral survey report was given to the supervisors for further guidance.

Think and Do

> "*Think of setting up community development projects for social work practice to create your own employment, and to render social services to get recognition, social status and respect in the society.*"

Chapter 7

Social Functions

"Effective public speaking is possible only if it is practised consciously."

Introduction

Well-established voluntary organisations and institutions organise social functions on different social issues based on the needs of the community from time to time in different cities and towns. Generally, theoreticians, practitioners, thinkers and needy persons, i.e., beneficiaries, are involved in such functions. The organisers could be, trained or voluntary social workers. Social functions pertaining to different fields of social work are always valuable. Therefore, such functions are to be utilised by the schools of social work for the purpose of fieldwork training. Maximum numbers of students must be sent to attend these functions. These students should be asked to collect relevant and useful literature pertaining to the fields of social work. The students deputed for such functions should be guided by experts and experienced persons. The following objectives of participation will be of great use in this regard.

Objectives of Participation in Social Functions

The major objectives to depute the students to participate in the social functions organised by local or outside social agencies are:

- To provide an opportunity to the students to interact with different personalities working in different fields of social work for the purpose of extensive training in social work.
- To make the students aware of the scope of social work profession, which will help them build their career in social work.

- To assist the students to improve their communication skills through dialogues with experts and delegates.
- To provide an opportunity to the students to gain exposure to varied experiences, and also to collect new information from different people.
- To help the students to develop their interest and zeal, on deputing them in different and new places which will enable them to understand fieldwork in depth.
- To develop the all-round personality of the students.

Preliminary Preparations

Students deputed to attend social functions should study the purpose of deputation prior to their actual participation in such functions. This will enable them to learn practical aspects. Students should bear in mind that such opportunities will not come again and again, and they should not miss these. Besides learning the objectives, they should read relevant literature, and try to analyse the matter studied. This preliminary preparation will help them to grasp the matter better. However, discussions with the faculty members will enable them to learn practical aspects in a better way.

General Practices in the Schools

Generally the schools of social work depute one or two students for such social functions organised by outside NGOs or institutions along with some faculty members. Students should make the utmost use of such opportunities, discuss the theme of the function with the faculty members and collect maximum preliminary information for effective and active participation in the function. This enhances the self-confidence and courage of the students who can then try for optimum benefit from the programmes. Similarly, they should look out for any such functions organised by local NGOs and institutions and participate in the functions, officially if required or unofficially, on their own if the functions are open to all. However, the students should discuss the issues with the faculty members before attending and prepare themselves for active participation, because they will not gain much if they are only silent listeners. Fulfilling the objectives discussed earlier rests entirely upon the students themselves. Their active participation will yield better fruits.

Methods and Procedure of Learning

The participants (students) should collect the literature circulated, if any, by the concerned agencies and glance through it whenever they find time during the function which will enable them to understand the subject matter being dealt with by the speakers. The following methods may be followed for effective learning and grasping of the subject matter:

- Careful listening.
- Careful observation of discussion.
- Purposeful participation in the session.
- Interaction with co-participants and speakers.
- General observation, i.e., organisation, manners, etiquette, etc.
- Jotting down important notes from the speeches.
- Pondering over and analysing the subject matter discussed.

Students are required to cultivate certain habits for the purpose of their own development. Listening carefully is one of the good habits by which many things can be grasped and retained. This holds true not only for the function but their day-to-day life also, because knowledge can be gained from every person who comes in contact with them in the field, community, school or anywhere else at any time. Students should be careful listeners at least when they are undergoing training. While listening to the lectures of the experts they should also cultivate the habit of jotting down notes, because human memory is unreliable and after some time they may forget important points.

After the lectures of the experts are completed, a discussion on the subject will be initiated. Senior participants discuss the student's queries. The student participants should follow these interactions carefully, especially about the subject, language used, manner, style of presentation, the subject matter, etc. The gist of the discussions with questions and answers, if any, should also be noted down.

Besides listening to the discussions of the co-participants the students should also ask questions to the speakers to get clarifications on issues that they may not be clear about. These questions should be intelligent and practical. It is here that the preliminary study would come in handy. This will not only assist them in acquiring knowledge, it will even enhance their self-confidence, which may make effective speakers in future. Every opportunity is to be fully utilised.

Listening to the lectures, observing the discussions of co-participants and participation in the discussion forms part of the entire process of the discussion. Students should also not lose any opportunity to interact with the co-participants or speakers during the function or during the recess.

Besides this, the students should observe the functions in general, i.e., style of the speakers, methods of organisation of functions, manners, etc. All this will enable them to organise functions on their own either in the schools, agencies or elsewhere in future. They should study other incidental features like, banners displayed in the seminar hall or in the agency, posters exhibited in the agency, etc. This empirical study should then be practised in the field in future, otherwise the purpose of organising social functions and deputing the students would be meaningless.

Process of Training in the School

After the functions are over, the students should be asked to submit their observational reports based on the literature collected from the concerned NGOs, talks of experts, discussions with them, and the points noted during the functions. The faculty members of the respective schools should check these reports. If necessary, they should suggest certain changes, to make the report more comprehensive. Students should then prepare to present it in the school before the other students and faculty members. The following model report devised for the purpose may be referred:

Model of Report on Social Functions

1.	Name of the student	:
2.	Batch number	:
3.	Roll number	:
4.	Name of the agency which organised social function and number of days	:

5.	Whether deputed by the school or attended on his/her own	:
6.	Faculty members present with the student	:
7.	Theme of social function	:
8.	Papers circulated to the participants by the speakers or the agency	:
9.	Whether papers read by the student during or after the function	:
10.	Participated in function	:
11.	Notes prepared by the students	:
12.	Summary of the function	:
13.	Observation of the student	:
14.	Nature of practical knowledge gained through the function	:

Signature
(Student)

Classroom Seminars on Social Functions

Students should be asked to organise seminars under the supervision of the faculty members. Such opportunities help them to develop their organising capacity and skills. They should be asked to present their papers and views on the issues of the training that they had undergone in the social functions. After presentation of the papers, a discussion should be held among the students. This discussion should be made meaningful and useful. Students should be taught to be brief and to the point in discussions. However, rural students are found lacking in this regard. They must understand that without putting in the required effort during the process of learning, the expected development cannot take place.

Preparation of Seminar Reports

All students who attend the seminar (organised by the students who had undergone training in different social functions) should be asked to prepare short reports on the seminar. These reports should be made compulsory and must be used to evaluate their performance. The following model devised for the purpose may be referred to:

Report of School Seminar on Social Functions

1.	Name of the student	:
2.	Batch number	:
3.	Roll number	:
4.	Name of the agency which organised social function and number of days	:
5.	Theme of social function	:
6.	Summary of the function organised by outside agencies	:
7.	Observation of the students	:
8.	Nature of practical knowledge gained through the function	:
9.	Participation in the school seminar organised by the students	:
10.	Issues discussed	:
11.	Observation and comments of faculty members	:
12.	Non-participating students' observations	:

Signature
(Student)

Evaluation of Performance

Reports of the social functions and the classroom seminars submitted by the students should be checked by faculty supervisors immediately to evaluate performance, and marks should be allotted. In the moffussil areas, reports are not taken from the students. Considering the values of report writing from the fieldwork training point of view, the schools set up in these areas should start this practise for the benefit of the students.

Model of Self-Evaluation Report after Social Functions

1. Name of the student :
2. Batch number :
3. Roll number :
4. Place of function :
5. No. of days of the function :
6. Paper presented in the function and classroom seminar :
7. Participation in the function and seminar :
8. Suggestions recorded in the functions and classroom seminar :
9. Views expressed :
10. Performance of self :
11. Maximum marks deserved :
12. Give reasons in brief for above :

Remarks:

Signature (Faculty Supervisor)

Signature (Student)

Benefits of Participation

Students derive many advantages through this method of fieldwork training which are enumerated below:

1. Skill in presentation of the subject improves, which will help in developing oratory powers.
2. Social outlook and social perspectives of the students develop.
3. Opinions and views of students on social issues take shape in the process.
4. Fieldwork knowledge of the students are enhanced, which help in dealing with problems in a better way.

Think and Do

"To be a good speaker and writer, the inner urge is to be kindled."

Chapter 8

Study Tours

"*Study tour is not only fun but is a method of training through recreation, sightseeing and observations.*"

Introduction

A study tour is a part and parcel of the fieldwork training in social work education. However, the policies and the practices of imparting training through a study tour may vary from school to school. In some schools it is compulsory and in others it is optional. Unfortunately, not much importance is given to it in the examination system, due to which the participation of students is poor everywhere. In spite of this, tours are organised by the schools. Such tours are more like the tours of the degree schools, and have very little to do with fieldwork training.

To enable the students to be well versed in social work practices, schools should organise tours separately for the first and final year. A specific practical syllabus should be framed on the basis of the theory syllabus and the specialisations. Marks should be given which should be counted in the annual examinations.

A systematic and methodical arranged study tour has a subject, procedure and some techniques. While choosing the topics to be studied in practical situations those covered during the orientation and concurrent fieldwork should be omitted and remaining aspects must be covered. To encourage students to understand the realities in society, both sociological and social work aspects must be covered as far as possible. One or two important institutional visits should be organised. One or two ideal villages or ideal community development projects must be included. One or two ideal governmental and non-governmental, national or international funding agencies must also be included. Their office procedures, methods, social services and social work practices, and contributions to the society at large must be studied. Besides institutional topics, certain general relevant ideas may also be included, like socio-cultural changes in the places/regions visited, novel concepts, ideas and methods used by the people and activists there, exchange of ideas and exposure to group life.

Some general aspects like reservation of tickets and accommodations, purposeful learning programmes through group entertainment, counselling services in the tours on the basis of the strengths and weaknesses of students, etc., should also be paid attention to.

Objectives of Study Tour

The specific objectives of the study tour framed by authority should be explained. The students should also learn the core of the objectives, which will enable them to understand how to learn the practical aspects in a professional sense. The objectives of study tours in social work education are as follows:

- To provide an opportunity to the students to have a group experience, to express their views and to exchange ideas and concepts regarding social aspects and social life, for the proper understanding of the web of social relationships, as well as for enhancing their practical knowledge and developing their personalities by shaping their views and perspectives.
- To provide an opportunity to study the socio-cultural changes and values, social practices and phenomena, in different parts of the country to mould their social outlook and also for enhancing their practical knowledge of the society.
- To enable the students to meet eminent personalities in the field of social work and to interact with them, learn from their experiences, and methods, see how work is done in critical situations and pick up the skills required, and building their career in the field.
- To study different ideas of social development, sources of national and international funds, methods, techniques and skills used by people, in implementing different types of projects, and also to know and understand the research done by the scholars, scientists and the NGOs/institutions.

- To enable students to visit ideal villages, community development projects and social welfare organisations, social institutions, so that they can learn the relevant methods, techniques and skills.
- To understand the procedures and methods followed in different kinds of funding agencies in different parts of the country.
- To impart training in social work education through purposeful recreation, sight seeing, discussions in different places and atmospheres. To observe and collect information from various sources, etc.

Syllabus for Study Tour

Faculty members and students should keep in mind the objectives of the tours and prepare their training programmes on the basis of the guidelines provided by the school or university. Their theoretical syllabus may also be referred to while planning the programme and preparing the tour schedule because it will guide them in choosing the places, projects and organisations. Since there is no tour syllabus as such, nobody has any idea of what is to be studied during the tour. To help prepare a proper training schedule and efficiently utilise the money, labour, time and energy spent, the author has devised a model syllabus for reference, which is as follows:

(a) Study of the model of a unique social welfare organisation and its services, methods and techniques, sources of funds, etc., for solving complicated human problems and aiding social progress and development.

(b) Study of an ideal village and its impact on the quality of life of the beneficiaries and the community at large, contribution of the leaders, activists, social workers, their ideas, motivations, inspirations, methods and techniques, and sources of funds.

(c) Study of ideal community development projects and their impact on the community, the agencies of these projects, their sources of funds, methods and techniques used, aspects and areas covered, successes and failures.

(d) Study of ideal governmental, non-governmental and foreign funding agencies, their procedures and practices, eligibility conditions, orientation and limitations of the funds, format of the proposals, documents required for getting funds, and their social work supervision.

(e) Study of some exemplary individual social workers, voluntary workers, activists, leaders, their sources of inspirations, motivations, ideas, imagination, sources of funds, activities and programmes, methods and techniques, skills, devotion, contribution and professional achievements.

(f) Study of the social phenomenon in the toured places, regions, their cultural aspects, social institutions like caste panchayats, religious social services like *dharmshalas*, services to helpless, gram panchayats, their economic services, social change, *mahila mandals*, *tarun mandals* and cultural clubs, etc.

(g) Study of the development and, contributions of associations like the Rotary Club, the Lions Club, and such others in educational development, scholarship trusts, etc.

Methods of Training

The specific objectives of the study tour and the practical syllabus gives us an idea of the training schedule as well as the nature and scope of training through the tour but it may not be very revealing about how to learn practical aspects in the places toured. To do so the faculty members have to guide the students as to the techniques and methods of study. Without knowing the purpose of learning, the purpose of imparting training in professional course will not be served. The faculty members have to coach and assist the students to prepare a theory relevant to the tour programmes, and give them a general idea of the places proposed to be visited along with the subject matter to be studied there. Queries and doubts are bound to crop up and this theoretical preparation will help students in answering these doubts. Students should use the following techniques to collect information from the places which are to be visited:

- Observation and discussions,
- Interactions and collections,
- Documentation and recording, and
- Photographs and notings.

Organising Study Tours

The study tour should be organised by students under the guidance and control of the faculty members of the concerned school. All the students should be involved in the process of organising the tour, i.e., planning, coordinating, executing and returning home.

To begin with, the student leader should call a general meeting of the students either in the presence or in absence of the faculty members and discuss pertinent aspects pertaining to the proposed places/regions, number of days, approximate tour expenses, accommodations, proposed agencies and their addresses with phone numbers, contact persons and their addresses, routes, kilometers, maps, guides, etc. The views of the students should be sought. The student leader can get the work done by the group and all the required information needed for the purpose of organising the tour is to be gathered in detail.

A second meeting of the students may be called and all the faculty members invited this time to take decisions and finalise the programmes. Factors like manpower, money, duration, social institutions, good individual volunteers, social workers, community development projects, historical monuments, ideal social welfare organisations, national and international funding agencies, etc., must be taken into consideration at this stage. Committees can be constituted under the guidance and control of the faculty members:

- Committee for reservation of railway or bus tickets and concessions,
- Committee to obtain permission to visit the proposed institutions,
- Committee to arrange for guest lectures in the schools on tour,
- Committee to fix accommodation in the proposed places,
- Committee to conduct group discussions, prepare and display banners in the proposed places, organise common group conference after the tour, and
- Committee for purposeful recreation and practical studies.

Faculty members should be in charge of the committees for the sake of guidance and control. Meetings of sub-committees should be held often to examine the progress of work allotted to them. After completion of preliminary preparation the programme chart should be prepared and displayed on the notice board for the information of the concerned persons. The programme chart is an indication that the study tour of social workers is quite different from that of degree schools or other institutions. Practical training can begin in the premises of the school, and continue till the participants return and till a common group conference is organised to share their experiences. Besides this, faculty members and student leaders should frame rules and regulations for maintaining discipline and any violation should be penalised. A model tour programme format is given hereunder which can be referred to for convenience.

Tour Programme Chart

(1) General
- (a) Professor-in-charge :
- (b) Student-in-charge :
- (c) Number of days :
- (d) Places to be visited :
- (e) Tour schedule :
- (f) Mode of travel :
- (g) Material to be taken :
- (h) Approximate expenditure :

(2) Accommodation :

(3) Organisations to be visited :

(4) Subjects to be studied :

(5) Recreation :

Pre-Training Programme

Faculty members arrange guest lectures of experts after the preliminary preparations but before proceeding on the tour. Experts are invited to deliver lectures on relevant topics to help students in their practicals during the tour. The following topics may be useful for the purpose:

- Study tour and personality development,
- Organising a tour of the social workers,
- Tour and group life,
- Observations and recording in the tours, and
- Tour reports.

Equipments to be Taken

The participants should carry a small diary for recording their observations which is useful for writing reports and also for future reference. They are expected to record each and every aspect of the concerned agencies and the places so that they do not forget these. Photographs of important agencies and the inmates, work situations, social issues, social scenes, natural scenes as also the photographs of colleagues, classmates and VIPs may be taken. A camera is to be taken along for the purpose. The students are reminded here that photographs will be very useful when it comes to writing their reports apart from storing memories. A tape recorder may also be of use in recording important lectures by experts of the agencies.

Fieldwork in Places Toured

The process of fieldwork begins as soon as a study tour is organised. The students learn planning, organising, coordinating, executing and controlling activities in practical situations. Such fieldwork is not given to them during the orientation training and concurrent fieldwork training. Hence, the students are supposed to observe the entire process minutely and gain practical knowledge. Similarly, they should observe the following things in the agencies/places and collect information for analysis and interpretation:

- Study of wall pictures, if any,
- Specific phrases on social work, if any,
- Motivation of founders in setting up the agencies,
- Documents regarding history of establishing the agencies,
- Documents regarding programmes and activities,
- Collection of photographs, and
- Collection of information regarding sources of funds, use of funds, techniques, social change and development that have taken place, etc.

Field Practices

Every student participant should be given an opportunity to introduce himself and the team; to say the vote of thanks; to draft letters of thanks, of appreciation, for seeking permissions, to express his experiences and feelings, requests to make arrangements, etc. Every student needs help from the faculty to learn etiquette and manners, the skills of administration of programmes and of interacting with different people. These activities will normally not be found in any textbook nor taught as part of the curriculum. Students must therefore, realise the importance of learning these things during the tours.

Office Process to be Completed

Students must get permission letters from their parents and submit them in the school office along with their applications. A tour programme chart is given to the parents for their reference, and if they wish they may contact their children over the telephone. Similarly address and phone numbers of the students should be maintained in the tour file and the photocopies of the same must be kept in the school office. The faculty members must carry school letterheads and seals, and a letter from the principal for emergency use during the tour. The students must take their identity cards, and a copy of the list of the students duly signed by the principal and the railway or bus authority. The necessary general medicine kit should be taken along. While travelling in different cities, the students should take the required precautions and record the autorikshaw numbers, address and telephone numbers of the hotels/guest houses, etc.

Sharing Experience

After the students return, they should share their experiences of the day. Everyone should be asked to relate his/her experiences, by which they may be able to collect certain points which they might have missed. After exchanging their ideas, views, opinions the faculty members can assist them in analysing and recording the events in their tour diaries and then conduct cultural programmes and entertainment.

Tour Reports

The students are asked to have discussions every evening. All these views should be analysed under the guidance of the faculty members and the minutes should be recorded in the diaries meant for the study tour. Similarly, they should be taught to write a rough report on the syllabus they cover during the day. This practice will enable them to finish their work on time and after completion of the tour they can write their final report and submit it in the school well in time. The school should devise a model tour report to maintain a systematic record of activities and help them in preparing correct reports. Lack of experience in writing reports is a major hurdle and students are confused when it comes to presenting the reports. Incomplete reports are submitted or the clerical staff is asked to help. The outcome will naturally not be up to the mark. Students should take this work seriously as reports not only form an important aspect of social work education but also enhance presentation capabilities. The author has devised a model report for the reference of the students.

Model of Tour Report

1. Individual Information
   (i) Name of the student :
   (ii) Class
   (iii) Roll No. :
   (iv) Period : From ____ To ____
2. General Background : (Places toured, geographical, social, cultural, economical, etc., in brief)
3. Institutional Information : (establishments, leadership funds, programmes, methods techniques skills, contribution, beneficiaries, social change, development, etc.)
4. Community Development Project : (areas, aspects, funds, programmes, development, change, methods, techniques)
5. Village Information : (leader, motivation, work programmes, contribution, impact, research if any in brief)
6. National/International Funding Agencies : (organisational background, funding schemes, procedure, methods, limitations, scope, eligibility conditions, criteria, etc., in brief)

7. Cultural Information (ways of life, movements, changes, etc., in brief) :
8. Social Background (occupations, professions, religious and caste groups, and their predominance in particular occupation or professions, etc.) :
9. Group Life Experience (identification of strengths, weaknesses, actions, reactions and contributions of the students) :
10. General Remarks :

Signature (Faculty) Signature (Student)

Group Conference

A common group conference is organised by the students after returning from the tour to provide them with an opportunity to relate their experiences and exchange ideas and suggestions. This enables them to grasp or understand the points/aspects, which might have been missed by them. Similarly, the expression of some of them may assist the rest to learn the different outlooks or perspectives of the studies.

Evaluation of Training

After submitting the report of the group conference to the professor in charge of the tour, the next and final step is assessment of the students on the basis of their participation, initiative, leadership, studiousness, presentation, performance, sincerity and honesty, etc. For evaluation, the students are supposed to submit their self-evaluation reports and the author has made an attempt here to draft a model self-evaluation report which may be of help. It is as follows:

Self-Evaluation Report Model

–	Name	:
–	Roll number	:
–	Batch number	:
–	Tour area/region	:
–	Number of days	:
–	Participation in planning and organising the programme	:
–	Professional interaction with the co-passengers and experts	:
–	Use of observation and techniques	:
–	Use of discussion method	:
–	Nature of practicals	:
–	Studies of funding agencies	:
–	Study of ideal village	:
–	Utilisation of time for studies and entertainment	:
–	Narrate in brief the marks you deserve and why	:
–	Remarks	:

Signature
(Faculty)

Signature
(Student)

It is said that a well-organised study tour with definite objectives and goals is an effective method of training in social work education. But its utility depends entirely upon the students and faculty members.

Think and Do

"Be a good observer, take the initiative and participate in all the activities of the tour sincerely and imbibe everything in your personality."

Chapter 9

Rural Social Work Camps

"Social work camps help the students in understanding the core of rural life, their problems and needs, and help them in preparing a plan for social work practice and community development."

Background

Generally NSS units are present in almost all degree schools, and students are encouraged to join its activities as a part of co-curricular activities. Student who are interested are given admissions at once. These NSS units conduct various social service activities in the schools as well as in the field. Rural social service camp is one of the major activities of the unit. Different kinds of programmes chalked out by the programme officers are notified to respective schools from time to time. At the end of the academic year the programme officers prepare detailed reports and publish them in the respective school magazines. Conducting various activities, organising public functions, publishing news in papers and notifying these in the schools, etc., creates a pleasant social and fertile learning atmosphere for the students. In turn they learn practical aspects of social life in the society, directly as well as indirectly.

However, after graduation when these students take admission to professional courses in social work education and start undertaking similar activities in their fieldwork, they make the mistake of emulating the same patterns that they had observed during their association with NSS.

It should be understood by all students of social work that there is a conceptual difference between the rural social service camps of NSS units and the rural social work camps of schools of social work.

A comparison of the general objectives of both the camps shows that they are more or less the same and certain programmes of rural social work camps are similar to the rural social service camps. However the similarity ends here. Social service camps are but a small part of social work camp.

Social work is a profession and social service activities are included in it. Therefore, the methods of social work camps are unique to it and it is necessary to narrate the nature of social work camps and their specific objectives, to give students of social work a clearer understanding of social work camps.

Rural Social Work Camps

Social work camps are unique in nature and scope and are organised by the students under the guidance of the faculty members. They visit the proposed places and identify the needs and interests of the people through professional interactions. The probable participation and cooperation of people is judged and preliminary information is collected to chalk out need-based programmes. While preparing the camp programmes the faculty members keep in mind professional training and help to the community. Certain recreational programmes are also incorporated to ease the stress and strain that would otherwise result from the continuous mental and physical work that students will have to put in. It also motivates people to work more. To serve the purpose of the camps in a professional sense and to prepare the programmes well, the students should know the specific objectives of such camps.

Objectives of Social Work Camps

The objectives of social work camps may appear similar to those of the social service camps. However, it must be noted that the former are much wider in scope. It is very essential that students, especially those who have undergone NSS training earlier, read and understand these objectives clearly. The major objectives of social work camps are as under:

- To make the students understand the rural social system and community living.
- To study the rural social problems and approaches, and strategies of intervention adopted.

- To develop an understanding of the level of government intervention and its impact on people.
- To study the impact of technology and western culture on the lives of the rural community.
- To understand the working and influence of social institutions like joint family systems, marriages, caste panchayats and gram panchayats on the life patterns of people.
- To study rural organisations like *Tarun Mandals* (youth organisations) *Mahila Mandals* (women organisations.), sports clubs, etc., and their level of intervention, specially for social development.
- To gauge the effect of evil customs, bad habits, superstitions, age old traditions and the impact of these on their life patterns.
- To interact with people of different strata and gain practical knowledge, and develop skills in guiding and counselling with providing more effective solutions to problems.
- To help the students develop their sense of care and social responsibility by applying social work techniques like counselling.
- To assist the students in learning through the experiences in group living so as to develop their social responsibility.
- To acquire skills in planning, organising and implementing camp programmes with productive use of time, communication skills, working with team spirit, handling relationships and conflicts, seeking cooperation and coordination whenever required, administration, etc.
- To enable the students to identify the needs of the rural communities and provide them the professional information on setting up an NGO, preparation of the proposals, tapping of funds, organising fund raising campaigns, teaching them management, legal and general office procedures and methods, counselling, etc.

Differences between Social Service Camps and Social Work Camps

The above mentioned specific objectives of rural social work camps indicate their nature, extent and scope. The following are the differences between social work and social service camps:

Sr. No.	*Social Work Camp (MSW)*	*Social Service Camp (NSS)*
1.	Compulsory for first year students as a part of social work training.	Optional for degree level students.
2.	Students are given marks for their participation in camps.	Students are not given marks for their activities.
3.	Students organise social work camps.	Programme officers organise NSS camps.
4.	Surveys are conducted to identify the needs of the community to provide professional help to individuals, groups and community.	Surveys are not conducted for the purpose of identifying the needs of the community in order to provide professional help to the individuals, groups and community. It is for general knowledge and understanding only.
5.	Social work techniques, i.e., casework, group work, community organisation, social welfare administration, social work research and social action are used to render professional services.	No specific techniques of social services have been devised to render services to the community.
6.	Guidance is provided to office bearers of the NGOs like *Tarun Mandal*, *Mahila Mandal* and such other organisations regarding legal and administrative matters, programmes and funds.	No such activity is undertaken by the NSS units.
7.	Certain programmes like plantations, *shramdans*, medical camps, etc., are undertaken as a part of the service activities of the camp.	Plantations, *shramdans*, medical camps, lectures, etc., are the main activities of the NSS camps.
8.	Social services like plantations, *shramdans*, medical camps, etc., are rendered and their follow-up is practised giving a professional touch to the services.	The NSS units practise no follow-up.
9.	Different methods like exhibition of posters on social issues, staging street plays, organising rallies, *morchas*, etc., are used as tools for influencing opinion of the community regarding bad customs and wrong traditions.	No such methods are used for reducing the gravity and magnitude of social evils.

Cont'd...

Cont'd...

10.	Referral services are provided to individuals, groups, organisations, etc. for seeking solutions to typical problems, which do not get solved through the existing community resources.	No referral services are provided to individuals, groups or organisations.
11.	Counselling services are rendered to weaker sections, women, handicapped, etc.	Counselling services are not provided by the NSS students.
12.	Fund raising campaigns are organised to guide rural workers and also to strengthen their activities and services.	No fund raising camps are organised and no such help is provided.
13.	Training programmes are conducted in the camps to enhance the skills of rural youth in terms of setting up voluntary organisations, their management and administration programmes, etc.	No such training programmes are conducted.
14.	Visits are paid to the offices of social institutions like gram panchayat, caste panchayat, etc., for the purpose of practical study and to understand the changing roles of these institutions.	No visits are paid to offices of social institutions.
15.	Government schemes of rural development are explained to the people and they are encouraged in their implementation.	No such efforts are made.

Specific Training Programmes

The explanation regarding the influence of NSS activities on the perspectives of the participants of degree schools, the nature of professional rural social work camps, clarifications about the exact differences between rural social work camps and NSS camps, etc., will give a clear understanding to the students regarding their approaches, methods and programmes of rural social work camps. However, the programmes are not designed and practised professionally in India. To solve this problem, the author has devised a model programme, which may be useful for the purpose of planning:

Camp Programme: Example

• Social Survey	:	Nature and structure of social systems, socio-economic, socio-psychological, socio-political background of the community and their needs to be studied.
• Social Institutions	:	Visits and observational studies regarding joint families, marriage, caste panchayat, religious places etc.
• Social Organisations	:	Visits and observational studies of youth organisations, women organisations, sports clubs, trusts, associations, unions, farmers' associations, etc.
• Social Practices	:	Observational studies of social customs like dowry, superstitions, religious rituals etc.
• Social Problems	:	Observation of social problems, discussions on these and guest lectures organised.
• Governmental Organisations	:	Visits and observational studies of political organisations like offices of the gram panchayat, gram sevak, village accountant, etc., along with their functions, efforts, problems and needs.

•	Cooperative Institutions	:	Visits and observational studies of cooperative institutions like cooperative cash credit society, cooperative societies, cooperative rural business organisations, their functions, problems and needs.
•	Educational Institutions	:	Visits and observational studies of *balwadis*, schools, high schools, their functions and problems.
•	Health Organisations	:	Visits and observational studies of private and government health services, their functions, problems, efforts, needs, etc.
•	Scheduled Caste Colonies	:	Visits and observational studies of SC colonies their social conditions, their problems, needs, efforts taken so far by local bodies, etc. Restrictions on visits to public places like hotels, temples, etc. Observations of general practices like untouchability, attitudes of the upper caste and SCs.
•	Guidance Services	:	Governmental and non governmental schemes available for the rural populace, their

		procedures, implementation, especially in schools, health services, occupational services, special services to the physically handicapped children, etc.
• Professional Counselling Services	:	Counselling services to be rendered to help the needy on the basis of the observational studies of the team.
• General Awareness	:	On the basis of the observational studies informal meetings of people to be conducted to create awareness among them regarding their problems, rights, responsibilities, duties, social attitudes, evil impact of bad habits, social problems, etc.
• Information on Rural Development	:	Government schemes and their funds, non-governmental schemes and their funds like IRDP, Rural Hospital, RLEGP, DWCRA, OB, ARTS, ARSWSP, CRSP, mini-welfare schemes, rural reconstruction, etc., to be brought to the notice of the people. Lectures by experts to be organised, discussions

			conducted and all possible services rendered.
•	Need-Based Services	:	Shramdan, plantation, free medical camps, exhibition of posters on different issues, rallies, purposeful cultural programmes, educational competitions, essay competitions, film shows, fund training programmes, etc., to be organised.
•	Referral and Follow-up Services	:	Chronic health cases should be referred to the government hospitals and other such need-based services rendered regularly.
•	Guest Lectures on Crop Managements	:	Guest lectures to be arranged to inculcate a scientific attitude among the villagers, especially about managing crops, protecting them from excessive rains, storms, pests, insects, etc.

Preliminary Preparations for the Camp

Students now have an idea about the rural social work camps after studying the scope NSS activities, difference between social work and NSS camps, nature and the model social work camp programmes, etc. To organise such camps professionally however, is not an easy task. The following procedure will help them in the task:

- The general theoretical background of rural community work to be studied.
- The theoretical background of social survey procedures to be gone through.
- Discussion with faculty members especially on rural life and practices, and on methods of fulfilling the objectives of the camps must be held.
- Discussions should include plans, programmes, sources of funds, involvement of people in the programmes, collecting material, help of outsiders, their contacts, seeking cooperation, contacting experts for lecturers and as guests, etc.
- A general study of governmental and non-governmental schemes, their procedures, implementation, etc., to be made and collection of the material regarding schemes, address of the contacting persons and the like should be carried out.

Meeting of the Students and Faculty Members

After the preliminary preparation the student leaders should take the initiative and call a general meeting of the faculty members and all students of the first year. The faculty members should guide them based on their experience, knowledge, new ideas, concepts, policies, plans, regulations, allocation of task, explanation of roles, etc., in relation to the entire camp project and action plan. This assists the student leaders in preparing a programme chart giving the day, date, distribution of work, programmes, functions, etc. This programme is based on the objectives of the camp model programmes, discussions with the faculty members, interactions with the village leaders, the specified needs of the selected community, etc.

Preparation for the Inaugural Function

An inaugural function should be arranged by inviting preferably, the Sarpanch or Head of the village, as chief guest or president of the function. Invitation cards must be given to all social workers, activists, political leaders, village officers, school teachers, government primary health centre employees etc. Maximum attendance by the villagers should be ensured. The invitation may also be pasted on the notice boards of the concerned village. A notice may also be published in the local newspapers if possible. Care must be taken to invite all well-known personalities personally. To create the right atmosphere, the meeting place should be decorated well and the decorum of the function maintained. Everyone in the village should feel that it is their programme and it is organised for them only. All formalities of the function should be observed.

Inaugural Function of the Camp

The inaugural function should be started according to schedule. The campers and the faculty members should be sincere enough to make the function successful. Success comes only to those who do the work systematically and methodically, with the help, co-operation and meaningful participation, of the villagers. A well and systematically conducted inaugural function will certainly leave an imprint in the minds of the persons attending it. The objectives of the camp and its professionalism should be brought out clearly. This helps in creating the right atmosphere and will assist the camping team to instill a sense of confidence in the villagers that something useful for the rural community is being done.

Implementation of the Programmes

To implement the proposed programmes the students and the faculty members must form groups and the more active students should be nominated as group leaders. The work is distributed among the groups and the leaders get the work done. Students should follow the principles and philosophy of social work and must keep in mind virtues as well as shortcomings of people. This is possible because the students from different classes, castes and environment come together for a noble cause. Camp life teaches the principle of collective work and offers them an opportunity to display their cultural talents. They utilise skills they have acquired during routine social service and, observational and actual work experience study.

The groups may be given suitable names that would give them a separate identity and inspire them in their activities in a competitive manner. Group leaders should seek guidance from the faculty from time to time; the faculty members should take care to see that the group leaders initiative and enthusiasm is suitably channelised and not curbed. To maintain this enthusiasm at a high level, it is always better to form the groups on the basis of physical strength and aptitudes because effective implementation of the various programmes depends largely upon the initiative of the group leaders.

Procedure and Methods

To achieve the objectives of the camp, the students should be aware of the correct procedure and methods of performing the allotted work. Most of the times students don't apply themselves scientifically and professionally to the alloted work. In such instances the entire exercise becomes a fruitless waste of time, money and labour. The procedure of working in the camp are narrated here for the benefit of the students.

(i) Social Survey: Project-1

A social survey is undertaken by schools to understand the nature and structure of rural community as well as to evaluate social conditions. In general these surveys remain on paper only, and students do not learn much from them. Faculty members and students should be more serious about surveys and taking into consideration the training-cum-utility aspect of the survey, different methods should be followed and practised strictly. While preparing the interview schedule the objectives of the camps must be taken into consideration and based on them the questions set in a language spoken by majority of the people of the area. The language should be very simple and words easily understood. The students must seek guidance from their faculty members regarding selection of respondents and conducting their interviews, etc. Students will not be able to collect enough data by merely asking questions from the schedule. A rapport has to be established with the respondents to take them into confidence. However, establishing rapport in just 15 minutes or half an hour is not an easy task. Students have to learn such skills while collecting data. Knowledge of the subject is necessary so that they can explain to the respondents if need be. A professional attitude is a must while collecting data. It should then be analysed properly to draw conclusions. The students should also learn the most important aspect, which is the cause and effect, otherwise it becomes difficult to interpret data in the right sense.

Next comes the process of coding, editing, classification, tabulation, interpretation, conclusion and report writing. Systematic training is to be imparted for all this. Social survey is conducted to impart training to the students and also to collect first hand information from people. Unfortunately, data from surveys is hardly utilised for the purpose of planning and development of the community. A social work camp is conducted as one of the important training tools and it must be utilised to gain professional competence. To ensure this, a report must be written in a language understood by majority of the people. It must be sent to the responsible social worker of the functioning social agency of that village or area. This, however, will also not serve the purpose. Follow-up practices should be observed by the same students or the students coming to the course for next year and by the faculty members. Consultancy services have to be provided by the schools to enable the villagers to utilise the survey work for real development of the community. The following specimen interview schedule may be referred to while framing the schedule:

Specimen Schedule
Survey of the Rural Community

(A)	*Personal Data*	:	
	(i) Name of the Interviewee	:	
	(ii) Address	:	
	(iii) Age	:	
	(iv) Sex	:	Male/Female
	(v) Caste	:	
	(vi) Religion	:	
	(vii) Educational Background	:	Illiterate/Literate/Primary /Secondary/Higher Secondary/ Graduation/ Post-Graduation/ Professional Education
	(viii) Hobbies	:	Reading/Writing/ Knitting/Collection of Articles/Cinema/Drama
	(ix) Habits	:	Drinking/Gambling/ Chewing Tobacco/ Eating Betelnut/Sunf

(B) *Family Data*

(i) Information about the family :

S. No.	*Name*	*Age*	*Sex*	*Education*	*Hobbies*	*Habits*
1.						
2.						
3.						
4.						
5.						

(ii) Total no. of family members :

(iii) Occupation of the family : Agriculture/Agri. Worker/Industrial Worker/Trade, Business/Service

(iv) Total annual income : Rs.

(v) Average monthly income : Rs.

(vi) Monthly expenses of family : Rs.

Itemwise details

(a) Foodgrains : Rs.

(b) Clothes : Rs.

(c) Medicines : Rs.

(d) Transport : Rs.

(e) Education : Rs.

(f) Recreation : Rs.

(g) Religious rituals : Rs.

(h) Guest : Rs.

(i) House rent : Rs.

(j) Social and incidentals : Rs.

(k) Habits : Rs.

Total : Rs.

(vii) Total Annual Savings : Rs.

(viii) Average Monthly Savings : Rs.

	(ix) Forms of Saving	:	Chit Fund/Cash Credit Society/Bank/Post Office/Insurance/UTI/(mention others)
	(x) Savings for children's Edn.	:	Rs.______/Not saved
	(xi) Savings for children's marriage	:	Rs.______/Not saved
	(xii) Any loss of income due to natural calamities (specify)	:	Year, Rs.
	(xiii) Impact of above on economy	:	Indebtedness/No Progress/Low Standards of Living
	(xiv) Loans/debts	:	Rs.
	(xv) Type of loan in details		
	(a) Crop loan	:	Rs.
	(b) Pipeline loan	:	Rs.
	(c) Loan for digging well	:	Rs.
	(d) Tractor loan	:	Rs.
	(e) Marriage	:	Rs.
	(f) Education	:	Rs.
	(g) Construction of house	:	Rs.
	Total	:	Rs.
	(xvi) Plans to repay the loan	:	
(C)	*Housing Condition*		
	(i) House	:	Rented/Owned
	(ii) No. of rooms in the house	:	2/3/4/5/5 and above
	(iii) Separate bathroom	:	Yes/No
	(iv) Separate latrine	:	Yes/No
	(v) Electricity connection	:	Yes/No
	(vi) Water facilities	:	Yes/No
	(vii) Type of house	:	*Kachha/Pacca*
(D)	*Living Standards*		
	(i) Have you got minimum furniture in the house?	:	Yes/No
	If yes, give details	:	Cot/Table/Chair/Stool/Sofa Set/(mention others)

	(ii) Convenience in the house	:	Gas/Gobar Gas/Stove/ Heater/Water Heater/ Mixer
	(iii) Have you got vehicles	:	Yes/No
	If yes, give information	:	Bicycle/Motorcycle/ Scooter/Four-Wheeler/ Tractor
	(iv) Means of recreation at home	:	Tape Recorder/TV/ Radio
	(v) Own sufficient clothes	:	Yes/No
	(vi) Composition of daily food food	:	Milk/Butter/Ghee/ Eggs/Mutton/ Vegetable/Pulses/ Sweet
(E)	*Occupational Information*		
	(i) Do you own a farm	:	Yes/No
	(ii) Total area	:	
	(iii) Nature of soil	:	Black/Red
	(iv) Type of crops produced	:	Cash Crop/Ordinary crops
	(v) Do you have latest cultivating equipment	:	Yes/No
	(vi) Agricultural method adopted	:	Traditional/ Mechanised
	(vii) Do you use improved seeds	:	Yes/No
	(viii) Do you use insecticides	:	Yes/No
	(ix) Do you get multiple crops	:	Yes/No
	(x) Is agricultural income sufficient	:	Yes/No
	(xi) Any additional occupation other than agriculture	:	Yes/No
	If yes, specify	:	
	(xii) Do you own animals	:	Yes/No
	If yes, specify	:	Cows/Buffaloes/ Bullocks/Horse/Goats

(F)	*General Information*		
	(i) Roads	:	Good/Ordinary/Bad
	(ii) Schools	:	Primary/Secondary
	(iii) Medical	:	Clinics/Hospitals
	(iv) Water	:	Tap/Well/Tank/River
	(v) Latrines	:	Individual/Community/ No Facilities
	(vi) State of latrines	:	Good/Fair/Bad
	(vii) Urinals	:	Yes/No
	(viii) Library	:	Yes/No
	(ix) Bhajan mandals	:	Yes/No
	(x) Drama Halls	:	Yes/No
	(xi) Cinema (tents)	:	Yes/No
	(xii) Gymnasium	:	Yes/No
(G)	*Social Information*		
	(i) Give detailed information of public institutions in your village	:	Gram Panchayat/ Cooperative Society/ Purchase-Sale Society/ Dairy/Primary Health Centre/Any Other
	(ii) Are you a member of any public institution	:	Yes/No
	(iii) Facilities available in the village	:	Bazaar/ST Stand/ Grocery Shops/ General Stores/ Workshops/Post Office
	(iv) Any social projects undertaken with the help of the people	:	Samaj Mandir/ Temple/School/Gram Panchayat/Recreational Centres
(H)	*Social Organisations*		
	(i) Any social organisations in the village	:	Yes/No
	If yes, specify	:	*Tarun Mandals/Mahila Mandals/Balbhavans/* Sport Clubs/Trusts/ Associations/Unions
	(ii) Are you a member of any of these organisations	:	Yes/No

(iii) Do you know the functions of these organisations : Yes/No

(I) *General Problems*

(i) Latrines and Urinals :

(ii) Waste disposal :

(iii) Drinking water :

(iv) Roads :

(v) School building, library, etc. :

(vi) Medical services :

(J) *Social Problems*

(i) Is dowry system practised in your village : Yes/No

(ii) If yes, do you practise it : Yes/No

(iii) Any dowry victims : Yes/No

(iv) Any alcoholic patients : Yes/No

(v) Is untouchability practised : Yes/No

(vi) Are public places open to lower caste people : Yes/No

(vii) Any juvenile delinquency in the village : Yes/No

(viii) Is family planning practiced : Yes/No

(ix) Any widowhood and divorcee problems : Yes/No

(x) Is child marriage practiced : Yes/No

(xi) Is continuous work available to landless labourers : Yes/No

(K) *Developmental Work*

(i) Is developmental work undertaken : Yes/No

(ii) Type of developmental work undertaken, specify :

(iii) Help received from which agency for the development of the village	:	Government/Zilla Parishad/ Rich people/ Villagers/Others

(L) *Need of the Community*

(M) *Additional Information*
Population :

(N) *General Findings*

(O) *Action Plan*
(on the basis of discussions)

Signature (Group Leader)	Signature (Faculty Member)

(ii) Social Institutions: Project-2

To understand the nature and structure of the social institutions in rural parts of the country, students must visit social institutions like religious trusts, temples, caste panchayats, church councils, mosques, marriage bureaus, joint families, single parent families, nuclear families, dharamshalas, and such other social institutions to study the functions, rules and their impact over the social behaviour and social relations of the people. They will be able to learn how social control is maintained by these traditional social institutions.

For this type of study, the students should find and contact the concerned persons, knowledgeable senior citizens and interact with them to collect reliable and correct information from them. The faculty members should give them certain points for systematic and to-the-point discussions. All this information must be recorded in the interview guide. Literature prepared by these offices should also be collected to find out relevant information, phrases, thoughts, philosophy of saints, if any, displayed on the walls of the offices of these different institutions should also be collected. An effort should be made to understand their impact over the social behaviour of people and whether the personalities of the rural people have changed because of these. Social information, like increase in social cohesion attributed to celebration of festivals together by different castes, religions, etc., should be obtained from the people. On the basis of these observational studies the faculty members should organise individual and group conferences and the students should be given an opportunity to express their feelings, views, opinions and to exchange their experiences gained through the observational group studies done while living together.

With the help of this analytical information, an article should be written in the local newspaper which will help to create awareness among the people about the positive role of the institutions. Similarly, collection of information regarding different social institutions assist the trainees in providing professional help right from giving latest information like changes taking place in the rural community, art of adjusting in these changing value systems and also for nurturing and developing social institutions. Besides this, information, guidelines and counselling services, regarding sources of funds like local, individual, institutional, Indian, foreign, etc., may be given by the students and the faculty members to the villagers. The schools of social work could get the following format copied for recording points of observation, collected information, literatures, etc.

Record of Observational Studies

Sr. No.	*Date*	*Title of the Programme*	*Name of the Institution Visited*	*Names of the Persons who Furnished Information*	*Particulars of Information Collected*
1.					
2.					
3.					
4.					
5.					

(iii) Social Organisations: Project-3

In order to learn and understand the nature and structure of the social agencies set up by voluntary workers in a village, students should visit social agencies like *Tarun Mandals*, *Mahila Mandals*, sports clubs, child guidance clinics, cultural centres, trusts, associations, unions, etc., and collect necessary information about their legal, social and economical status, management, administration, fieldwork programmes, beneficiaries, participation, difficulties, their impact on the people and community at large.

Such information can be collected from discussions, observations and literature, which can then be analysed and conclusions drawn about various social agencies and their functions. This will throw light on their efforts and needs.

On the basis of this first hand information, the students and the faculty members should call a meeting of the office bearers of these agencies and a training programme should be chalked out for them as well as the youth. This programme should be about methods of running existing agencies as well as setting up new ones. Imparting systematic training to the young voluntary workers and non-participant youth on methods and procedures of initiating new agency set-ups, collecting funds, setting up social agencies and running them is a must because generally they do not have access to such scientific knowledge. Such professional training will motivate them to implement various rural projects devised by the state and the central governments.

Besides this, a list of Indian as well as foreign funding organisations should be given to them so that they will be able to study funding problems of their project, find solutions and implement them. To encourage their participation a small fund-raising programme may be organised, by which the students will also learn and the villagers will derive benefit from it. The faculty members should guide them in every step. For their preliminary practical guidance the following books may be referred to:

- The Societies Registration Act, 1860.
- The Public Trust Act, 1952.
- Council for Advancement of Peoples Action and Rural Development.
- SOSVA POST (Magazine).
- Government Schemes.
- Fund Raising: A SOSVA Publication.

Faculty members should conduct individual and group conferences after all these activities are finished.

Students should be asked to write reports about the entire project, the data collection meetings, etc. The format for recording the work is as follows:

Record of Studies and Activities of Social Organisations

Sr. No.	*Name of the Agencies Visited*	*Name of the Officers with whom Discussed*	*Subject of Discussion*	*Type of Training Imparted*	*No. of Participants*
1.					
2.					
3.					
4.					
5.					

(iv) Social Practices: Project-4

Various customs, traditions and usages as well as superstitions and blind beliefs are practised in rural parts of the country. Certain customs and superstitions have been responsible in keeping the people backward. People are unable to come out of the influence of the customs and superstitions easily because these have been practised for thousands of years. Their illiteracy and ignorance are the main reasons for continuance of these practices. Moreover, such practices can not be stopped in a d ay. It is a long process. Social work students should take up projects to stop these practices during their rural camps. This is a very difficult project, and to make it easy, the students could go through relevant literature.

Once the preliminary preparation is done by the students, they can organise a few programmes on important issues as under:

- Dowry system and dowry deaths.
- *Purdah* (veil) system and social movements.
- Celebrating festivals, rituals, etc., by taking loans on interest.
- Praying to God for children.
- Praying to God to treat the ill and appeasing him with animal sacrifices.

The students should display posters indicating the evil effects of these systems and practices, and organise rallies in the village with slogans, stage street plays on such issues, arrange cinemas, conduct meetings of the people, arrange guest lectures, etc. However, merely doing such programmes in the village is not enough.

Voluntary workers of the village should be motivated to conduct such programmes every now and then. For that the schools should provide consultancy services because continuity is a must, otherwise the time, money, and labour will go waste. Follow-up practices should generally be observed. Changing of public opinion is a long process. Social change does not come on its own or in one or two programmes. The villagers should be guided, encouraged and motivated for the purpose. The following format may be referred to for recording purposes:

Record of Information and Activities of Social Practices

S. No.	*Name of the Programme*	*Particulars of Work Done*	*Methods Used for the Purpose*	*Participation of the People*
1.				
2.				
3.				
4.				
5.				

(v) Social Problems: Project-5

Social problems are the direct outcome of social disorganisation. They are prevalent not only in our modern society but in the traditional societies as well. Social thinkers and scientists are studying these problems and trying to evolve practical suggestions for them. The government is also spending crores of rupees in conducting researches, but in spite of these sincere efforts the problems have not been eradicated. The hard truth is that social problems cannot be eradicated completely. Their spread and magnitude can only be reduced. Generally, problems arise when changes take place in society.

Generally social action as a technique of social work has not been used or practised for solving social problems. Therefore, such techniques must be used as social surveys, interactions, meetings, exhibition of posters, organising rallies, staging street plays, arranging expert lectures, showing films, imparting social education, conducting research activities, etc. with the help of these the social workers should mobilise public opinion on the evil effects these problems on the society. The burning issues should be taken up first and then one by one the other problems can be handled. Students should bear in mind that the gravity of the problems cannot be reduced immediately after their intervention. It is a slow and long process and continuity is to be maintained otherwise the efforts will go waste. Arranging programmes every now and then is not possible for the students, hence, the people themselves are to be motivated to carry out such programmes in the future. Consultancy services should be provided to them whenever required. After completing the devised programmes the faculty members should conduct individual and group conferences of the students. To record their work the following format may be used.

Record of Activities on Social Problems
Training-cum-Social Work Programmes

S. No.	*Particulars of Work Done*	*Participation of the People*	*Initiative Taken by the Localites for Future Programme*	*What the Student Learnt*
1.				
2.				
3.				
4.				
5.				

(vi) Governmental Organisations: Project-6

Governmental organisations such as Gram panchayat, Taluka panchayat, Zilla parishad, etc., play vital roles in the development of rural areas of the country. Their roles, both, from theoretical and practical point of view should be studied.

The government establishes different offices in every village, i.e., Gram panchayat, village accountant, Gram sevak and provides other facilities to the villagers. Students of social work should study the use of such facilities made by the people and their positive and negative impacts. They must also see whether development has taken place in the community, the problems and difficulties of the offices, malpractices, etc.

For this, They must visit these offices and interact with the concerned officers and the employees, leaders of the village and a few common people and collect the necessary information. Based on this information different awareness programmes should be implemented. Methods like case studies, counselling, meetings, group conferences, lectures, etc., may be used and the concerned officers should be made aware of their roles, responsibilities, etc. To record the information collected and note the activities conducted the following format may be used:

Record of Information and Activities of Governmental Organisations

Sr. No.	*Information Collected in Brief*	*Programmes Implemented*	*Guidelines to the People*	*Participation of People*	*What Students Learnt*
1.					
2.					
3.					
4.					
5.					

(vii) Cooperative Institutions: Project-7

The philosophy of cooperation emerged from the needs of the people. The start of social living can be attributed to the necessity of people to cooperate with each other. The theory of cooperation is a must in all walks of life. Systematic cooperative movements over the years have brought about tremendous change in the society.

To develop any community therefore different kinds of co-operative institutions are established. Some villages and towns have turned into big industrial cities due to these co-operative movements. The philosophy of cooperative movement is to be understood well by the cooperative body members and shareholders. An honest and able leadership is required who also has long vision and perspective so that this movement is successful.

Considering the significance of cooperative movements and the need for their proper development, small cooperative units established in the villages should be studied and the necessary information collected. Different methods of observation and discussion should be used consciously. The students should visit all the small co-operative units like co-operative cash credit society, co-operative milk dairy, co-operative multi-purpose society, co-operative society, co-operative business and trade centres, etc. The efforts, successes, difficulties, problems, leadership, etc., of these societies must be studied and awareness generating programmes implemented accordingly.

Public opinion is to be mobilised in favour of co-operative movements. To do this, different methods like individual conference, group conference, informal meetings, guest lectures, pasting slogans indicating the importance of such movements, exhibitions, etc., should be used and a conducive atmosphere should be created in the village. The leaders working in the field should be encouraged and motivated to extend their co-operation. The social philosophy of involving people of different strata, caste, religion, etc., in the movement should be inculcated in the personalities of people. Professional help should be provided to them in this regard.

Merely creating an atmosphere is also not enough to establish this movement or to make it successful. Follow-up practice is a must and since the students cannot do this all the time, the locals must be motivated to carry on the good work. The schools should make consultancy services available to the people. The co-operative department of the government can provide them the necessary information, guidance and services but creating awareness among the people regarding the movement, their rights, duties, practices, malpractice, etc., can be done effectively only by the social workers. Faculty members and students should be able to render services in this regard.

To record the information collected by the students during the field visits and the programmes done by them, the following formats may be used:

Record of Information and Work of Co-operative Movement

S. No.	*Information Collected*	*Programmes Implemented*	*Participation of the People*	*Future Plans*	*What Students Learnt*
1.					
2.					
3.					
4.					
5.					

(viii) Educational Institutions: Project-8

Education is one of the most important contributing factors to social development but is neglected in the rural parts of the country. Peasants do not give much importance to the education of their children because they are asked to work in the fields especially during the harvest seasons. School drop-out rates are high in rural areas.

State government, Corporation and Zilla parishad schools are established in most villages. Often it is seen that the primary school teachers of villages do more non-teaching work than teaching work. An inspection of the schools is conducted every now and then for the mere sake of doing it. Senior citizens of the villages also do not focus their attention towards the school and teaching work. The pupils are automatically sent to higher classes without judging the capabilities. Their foundation is, thus, not strong, as it should be.

In some places school betterment committees are constituted by the villagers but they do not function properly. The concerned teachers commercialise this work instead of regarding it as their profession. The condition of the school buildings is also dilapidated. The rich manage to send their children to good schools in cities but the children of the poor undergo training in such an atmosphere. Taking into consideration this position of educational institutions in rural areas in general, a survey should be done by the students of social work during their camp which would enable them to highlight the weaknesses of these institutions. Proper guidance and counselling services can then be rendered to the poor villagers about education of their children. Programmes can also be implemented to satisfy the basic educational needs of the villagers.

The following educational programme guidelines can be undertaken in the selected villages:

- Formation of a school betterment committee.
- School building and repair.
- Fund raising programme and people's participation.
- School discipline and school health project.
- Organisation of meetings of the teachers and parents.
- Conducting free coaching classes and involvement of experienced retired teachers in it.
- Conducting adult education classes.

- Organising social education and training programmes for the same.
- Setting up *balwadis*, high schools and vocational schools.
- Forming teams for guidance and counselling.
- Awareness generation programme.

In order to make these programmes effective, students and faculty members should use their management skills and ideas to illustrate the government schemes and their procedures. Villagers must be motivated to implement schemes of the state and the central governments, voluntary organisations, individual workers, etc. To bring professionalism into this work, self-reliance, self-development, self-awareness, self-help, self-ability, etc., should be taught to people. People should be able to make their own decisions towards satisfying their needs.

Motivation should be provided by the students and faculty from time to time and consultancy services rendered whenever needed. Students and the faculty members should gather all the necessary information from the government offices and all schemes like DWCRA, CRSP, RLEGP, AES, NSRY, IP, NFE be studied in detail.

The following format may be used to record data:

Record of Educational Activities

Sr. No.	*Identified Programmes and their Implementation*	*Particulars of Work Done*	*Participation of the Villagers*	*Proposed Projects in Future*	*Expected Consultancy Services*	*Remarks*
1.						
2.						
3.						
4.						
5.						

(ix) Health Organisations: Project-9

The condition of health in the villages is pathetic. Birth and death rates are very high, infanticide cases are high, there is inadequate food, people live in unhygienic conditions and there are no proper arrangements for improving these conditions. Health facilities and services are not available because mostly unqualified and unregistered practitioners are present in rural private dispensaries.

Besides the poor health conditions prevailing in the villages, the people also believe in superstitions and blind beliefs, which add to the deteriorating conditions of health.

To improve health services, the students and faculty members should study the availability of private dispensaries, qualified doctors, registration, facilities, services, government health centres, co-operative hospitals, etc., and a small survey may be conducted to judge the health habits of the people, diseases, health expenses, etc. This will shed light on the actual health in the village and it will enable the students and the faculty members to plan out the possible services to be rendered. The following health programmes can be referred to.

- Setting up projects of socialisation of medicine,
- Setting up a rural co-operative hospital,
- Utilisation of primary health centres,
- Awareness generation programme,
- Organising free medical check-up camps,
- Arranging mobile van and dispensary,
- Setting up of co-operative medical shops,
- Ensuring availability of blood for emergency and
- Implementation of government health schemes.

The social work students and faculty can help by acquiring information related to the following:

- Central and state government schemes,
- Health without doctors,
- Literature prepared by SOSVA, Pune,
- The Co-operative Registration Act,
- Loan facilities for health and health insurance, and
- General health literature.

The proposed health programmes must be implemented with the help of following methods:

- Exhibition of posters on health,
- Organising rallies on health issues and needs,
- Arranging guest lectures by experts,
- Staging street plays,
- Case studies and casework, and
- Conducting informal meetings, public meetings, etc.

It is necessary to create an atmosphere of confidence in the village so that people can carry on the above mentioned programmes in future also under the guidance of the school of social work. Besides, this also helps the students to develop co-operative attitudes in the people. In turn, people may themselves set up either co-operative hospitals or schemes of socialisation of medicine which can be developed in future with some financial assistance from private funding organisations, governmental or foreign funding organisations. For the scheme to materialise socialisation of medicine is one of the best ways and it is rather easy to implement immediately, on a self-help basis. The procedure to start this scheme is as under.

Considering that Rs. 25 is the average monthly expenditure of family, and it is collected, the total collection from say 500 families will amount to be Rs. 12,500 within this amount, one qualified doctor, one assistant and a social worker can be appointed and the required basic medicines purchased. Associations of medical representatives and primary health centres could be approached and maximum quantity of free medicines can be collected from there. With all these a fairly well-equipped dispensary could be set up in the village. For specialised treatment, the social worker can take the patients to government hospitals in the city. Qualitative services can, thus, be provided to them. After sometime some special health scheme of the government may be implemented and a rural hospital set up. In the same manner co-operative hospitals can also be set up. The remaining programmes can be conducted from time to time by the villagers, however, motivation should be given for the same and the schools should render consultancy as well as referral services. The following format could be provided to the students for recording the work done by them.

Record of Health Activities

Sr. No.	*Particulars of Work Done*	*Participation of the Villagers*	*Proposed Future Plans*	*Expected Services*	*What Students Learnt*
1.					
2.					
3.					
4.					
5.					

(x) SC & ST Colonies: Project-10

Caste system is an integral part of rural community. Value patterns are predominantly caste-oriented and as a result people have become narrow-minded and want to preserve the interests of their own caste. This creates obstacles in the path of progress and development.

Even though a number of laws have been enacted to solve the problems of SCs and STs, the condition of these people is miserable and inhuman. The so-called superior caste people treat them very badly. Government policies and facilities too have not brought about the expected change among the people. Therefore, it falls upon trained professional social workers to render services in selected villages and initiate a change in people's attitudes.

Students must therefore pay a visit to the SC and ST colonies, to identify and record the practices of untouchability, practised overtly or otherwise. Suitable programmes of social work practices must be chalked out and efforts should be made to bring all leaders, politicians, social activists, senior citizens and concerned government officials on a common platform for the purpose. Organising guest lectures, group discussions, informal meetings, rallies, staging street plays, arranging exhibitions, etc., will definitely assist the social work students in creating an atmosphere in which people will feel that a change can be expected. This also will motivate them to further the cause on their own. Conducting of camps and the presence of social work students will encourage and motivate youth and women's organisations to continue these programmes. To ensure, this, proper guidance in terms of funds, management, etc., should be provided and referral services given so that they may be able to contact the consultants for future programmes.

Record of Activities on SC and ST Colonies

Sr. No.	*Title of Programme*	*Particulars of Work Done*	*Participation of the People*	*Initiative Taken by People for Future Programmes*	*What Students Learnt*
1.					
2.					
3.					
4.					
5.					

(xi) Guidance Services: Project-11

Village folk, in general are unaware of governmental and non-governmental schemes and facilities. They are not able to utilise them for their personal and social development. Hence, the students of social work camping in the villages should help the community to help themselves. They must give guidance about different existing schemes of the state and central government and their procedures and methods. The students must be knowledgeable enough to be able to provide help. The SOSVA, Pune, or offices of different ministries especially Ministry of Rural Affairs will be of help in this matter to the students. The collected material should be studied to understand the official technical procedure. Discussion with government officers and faculty members will also aid them in offering significant information to the villagers and help them in utilising suitable schemes.

(xii) General Awareness: Project-12

Illiteracy is rampant in rural areas of the country. This breeds ignorance in people. They are not aware of their rights and responsibilities, social duties, their social problems and the resultant evil effects on the society, etc. All these contribute to lowering their living standards. To enhance their social life it is necessary to create awareness in them. But since the student campers will be camping in these parts only for 10 to 15 days, it is not possible for them to achieve the targets of creating awareness within such a short period of time. Therefore, youngsters, leaders, and activists in the village should be taught through group discussions, lectures, posters, rallies, street plays, etc.

(xiii) Counselling and Referral Services: Project-13

Certain problems of the rural people are not solved effectively, especially those relating to their traditional living patterns and practices. Their belief in traditional systems and the age old ways of tackling problem is firm. They are not aware of the changing techniques and skills of solving problems. Hence, it is the duty of the student campers to make them aware about such services and their significance. The necessary information about trained social workers, NGOs and such other centres should be provided to them.

This will definitely help them to seek counselling services. Similarly, a few case studies could be made and professional counselling services rendered to them. The students must help the villagers to help themselves.

(xiv) Need-Based Social Services: Project-14

Student campers should render social services like shramdan, plantation, etc., and organise certain health camps, like eye camps, general health camps, etc. This will help the villagers and students realise the significance of dignity of labour. Students must ensure follow-up practice either directly or through local organisations.

(xv) Guest Lectures: Project-15

Guest lectures by experts on important issues like management of crops and saving them from excessive rains, storms, pests, insects, droughts, etc., will teaches villagers crisis management. Such services are to be rendered by students. To make the lecture halls attractive, posters should be exhibited on relevant topics. Similarly, lectures on agricultural development, rural development, community development, social development, should also be arranged to make the people more development-oriented.

Valedictory Function

Student campers should take the initiative to organise a valedictory function after completion of the camp programmes. An outsider should be invited as chief guest of the function. Generally politicians are invited for such functions. It would be better to invite professionals or rural leaders who have contributed to the rural development process in different projects. This will help in creating a suitable atmosphere of self-help and motivate the villagers to learn more. Student participants should also be asked to express their views and share their experiences with other campers and also with the guest. Similarly, the villagers should be asked to share their experiences too. Attending lectures of the guests, expressing views and sharing experiences in the programme will help the campers in moulding their views. Finally, all the concerned persons who helped in organising the camp should be thanked sincerely.

After coming back to school from the rural areas, student campers should write letters to all concerned officials and associates. Their professional relations will thus, be strengthened and a cooperative attitude will develop. The social work institution will grow, and earn the goodwill and professional recognition in the society.

Organisation of Seminar

Students should organise a seminar on camp activities. Trained and professional social workers may be called as a chief guest for the seminar. Students should present their papers written under the guidance of the faculty members and a discussion held on different dimensions of the rural system and problems. The chief guest may also guide the students in terms of rural living and rural social work. After this seminar students should be asked to prepare reports. Students may refer to the following format:

Model of Camp Report

(i) Name :
(ii) Roll number and batch number :
(iii) Location of camp :
(iv) Duration of camp :
(v) Camp leader (student) :
(vi) Camp coordinator :
(vii) Nature of camp activities :
(viii) Methods of social work :
(ix) Rural life observations :
(x) Practical experiences gained during the camp :
(xi) Participation of the students :
(xii) Cooperation and participation of the villagers :
(xiii) Interest of the villagers regarding social change :
(xiv) Nature of rural problems :
(xv) Difference experienced between NSS and social work camp :
(xvi) Views on camp :

(xvii)	Suggestions about camp activities	:
(xviii)	Guidance and cooperation of the faculty members	:
(xix)	Use of campers to the villagers	:
(xx)	Cost benefit analysis	:

Signature (Faculty) Signature (Student)

Evaluation of the Camp Programme

Schools of social work should evaluate and give marks for the performances of the student participants. Evaluation may be internal or external but it will be better if it is done in the presence of the students. However, to judge the performance the faculty members should ask the student participants to submit their self-evaluation reports.

Self-Evaluation Report Model

(i)	Name	:	
(ii)	Batch number	:	
(iii)	Area of camp	:	
(iv)	Number of days of camp or Duration of camp	:	
(v)	Present days/absent days	:	
(vi)	Reasons of absenteeism if any	:	
(vii)	Activities in which contributed	:	
(viii)	Services rendered	:	Organisation/Planning / Execution/Service/ Guidance/Counselling
(ix)	Activities in which he/she did not take interest, with reasons	:	
(x)	Methods and skills used for social service and social work	:	
(xi)	Total days of halt made and total hours worked	:	
(xii)	Practical experience gained during the camp programmes	:	

(xiii) Exemplary work done in the camp :
(xiv) Use of camp services for exam and its utility value for practice :
(xv) Practical aspects learnt in camp :
(xvi) Opinions and suggestions regarding the camp in general :
(xvii) Marks expected :
(xviii) Honest opinion of your own participation :

Signature (Faculty)	Signature (Student)

Think and Do

"Prepare an action plan of a small or big social work project and render services to the rural community as per your convenience or through an NGO, even if your field of work is different, and thereby contribute something to the well-being of your rural counterparts as an obligation to society."

Chapter 10

Fieldwork through Films

"Films too can teach you the realities of life."

Introduction

Practical training in social work education is offered through the different methods of fieldwork like orientation visits, concurrent fieldwork, guest lectures by practitioners, study tours, social camps, participation in social functions and in social movements, etc. These methods have become an integral part of the training programme today. Along with these, a new method of training through films has also been found to be very attractive and effective in developing the critical and analytical thinking of the students. In terms of understanding practical aspects of a social problem expressed through the emotions of actors and actresses, this method has no parallel. These are more meaningful to the students, who can develop necessary skills to work with people in practical situations. This method also inculcates a keen sense of responsibility among students, especially in moffussil areas.

Objectives of the Study

The major objectives of introducing this novel method of fieldwork training along with other methods are as under:

- To stimulate interest and zeal in social work students to perform practical work sincerely and honestly for their development, which in turn is beneficial to the society at large.
- To enhance the ability and capacity of students to relate the problems picturised in films with social work theory and

philosophy, and develop a critical and analytical thinking of social perspectives.

- To help students improve their discussion methods and expression powers.
- To help students form opinions and views on different aspects of social issues, as picturised in the films, and compare them to the actual theory and philosophy.
- To develop their practical knowledge through this method.
- To involve the students in an emotional learning process so as to enable them to accept new ways and change their traditional thinking.

To fulfil the specific objectives of fieldwork through films the following procedure of study has been suggested.

Procedure of the Study

Students learn theory and philosophy in classrooms, which develops their capacity to think. However, developing skills required to work with people, needs fieldwork practice. Fieldwork practice can be developed through different methods, and emotional learning through films is one of the most effective method. The social issue, that has been dealt with in the film, should first be explained to the students by the faculty supervisors. Specific guidelines should be given to them on the central idea of the film after which the film is shown. Discussions again follow after the screening is over.

Personal Group Discussions

A group discussion session should be conducted immediately after or on the day after the film show. Faculty supervisors should encourage the students to discuss on the issues in brief. After such discussions the faculty supervisors should explain the principles and philosophy of social work that have been used by the filmmakers in tackling the problem.

Report of the Study

Reports are prepared on the issues based on verbal explanation, film shows and the group discussions. Guidelines may be given to the students about report writing and the expectations of the emotional learning process. Such practices will enable them to express their view points on the central message of the story, and will develop their social perspectives. The following report devised for this purpose may be referred to. These reports should then submitted for record-keeping and evaluation purposes.

Report of Film Study

(i) Name of the student :
(ii) Name of the school :
(iii) Batch number :
(iv) Roll number :
(v) Film watched :
(vi) Theme of films :
(vii) Social aspect picturised in the film :
(viii) Social work principles and philosophies used :
(ix) Message given through the film :
(x) Impact of dialogues, songs, story and emotional expressions :
(xi) Theme and reality :
(xii) Social work or fieldwork :
(xiii) Knowledge gained through the film :
(xiv) Opinions and suggestions :

Signature (Faculty) Signature (Student)

Self-Evaluation Report

Reports prepared by the students have to be evaluated just like any other report and marks given for their quality. This will encourage the students to do their fieldwork sincerely. The report should be prepared according to the format given below:

Self-Evaluation Sheet

(i) Name of the Student :
(ii) Name of the School :
(iii) Batch Number :

(iv) Roll number :
(v) Name and theme of the film watched :
(vi) Social aspect or philosophy touched :
(vii) Message received from the theme, dialogue, songs, etc. :
(viii) Practical knowledge gained through the film :
(ix) Utility of knowledge for shaping the views, opinions and development of the personality :
(x) Opinions and suggestions regarding this method of study :
(xi) Marks deserved :
Faculty Remarks

Signature (Faculty) Signature (Student)

Advantages to the Students

People always like novelty and ideas which stimulate their inner urges. Similarly, this new method of learning through films effectively handles the urge of learning. Through this innovative method of fieldwork training the students can get the following benefits:

(i) Since a film addresses a social problem and its repercussions on the society through vivid visual presentations, it leaves a more lasting impression on the memory.
(ii) A different method of presentation of social problem is refreshing and a good change from the usual monotony.
(iii) Since this method also involves a discussion session after the screening, students can hone their observational and oratory skills.
(iv) This method also helps the students to develop their presentation styles, and in turn, this helps them to develop leadership qualities.

(v) Students can learn much faster ways to present their ideas, views, opinions, etc., by observing the effective characterisations in the films.

Films on Social Issues

Many films have been based on social issues. Some of the films discussed here are very relevant and useful for imparting practical training in social work education.

(i) Aatmavishwas (Marathi)

The meaning of *aatmavishwas* is self-confidence, which happens to be the core of casework. This film deals with the influence of one's confidence over the human mind and life and how a person can become problematic when he or she loses confidence. When self-confidence is regained the problems are solved. This film will certainly be useful to teach casework practically.

(ii) Umbaratha (Marathi)

This film deals with girls and women at a reception centre. It shows the nature and structure of mismanaged reception centres and the difficulties of girls and women admitted there. The positive aspects of management can be taught from this film.

(iii) Sparsh (Hindi)

Problems of the physically handicapped (blind) have been effectively portrayed in this film. It also dwells on the desires of the blind people and how they hate sympathy. Students can learn a lot when they get a chance to handle such cases.

(iv) Choukat Raja (Marathi)

This film deals with the problem of mentally retarded children. Effective picturisation and expression of the actors and actresses can help students to understand the problems of the mentally retarded in a much better way.

(v) Anjali (Hindi)

This film also deals with the problems of mentally retarded children. The wonderful performance of the little girl can teach a lot about the practical aspects of this social problem.

(vi) Mandi (Hindi)

This film deals with the life of prostitutes. The role of the pimp between the commercial sex workers and the customers, and the life pattern of the prostitutes has been depicted in the film.

(vii) Nikah (Hindi)

The central idea of the film is the problem of divorce among Muslims. The story and the message of the film can teach the students a lot about this social aspect.

(viii) Krantiveer (Hindi)

This film gives message to the public about self-help and self-reliance. The actor motivates people to help themselves to solve their problems.

Besides these there are many other films and documentaries which deal with some social issue or the other. Such films should be shown to the students for the purpose of practical training in social work education. This is the need of the hour because the students of moffussil area lack interest, zeal and they are more examination oriented even though social work is a professional and practical course. The hidden social message behind every film has to be elaborated and discussed so that students benefit in their practical social work.

Think and Do

"Watch films as a method of study and think over the issues from a social work point of view."

Chapter 11
Fieldwork Evaluation

"Evaluation helps to understand the weaknesses and strengths of the students in terms of professional competence."

Introduction

The evaluation of theory and practicals is normally done at the end of the academic year. Evaluation is an important tool of purposeful teaching and learning in social work education and it is done throughout the year right from orientation through placement and ends with the end of placement period, i.e. phase-wise, method-wise, period-wise, etc. The supervisors evaluate the performance of students regularly in order to decide the next step in teaching-training programme. These periodical supervisory sessions help the students to get an idea of the practical training and it also assists the supervisors to judge the knowledge and outlook of the students. The process is aimed at moulding students into trained professionals on the basis of standards established by the schools or university. Assessment of records, oral test, contribution in the agency, social outlook and perspectives, social work skills, etc., are judged. The schools should establish a process of assessing the students consciously as to what they have to do, what they have to learn to improve their skills, etc. It is important for the students to get a bearing of how far they have come and what they have learnt in the given period of time. In other words, it can be said that evaluation is not just an assessment of the present performance but is a review of the progress of student since the beginning of the placement.

Definition of Fieldwork Evaluation

Evaluation has a value to the client, the agency, the supervisor and most importantly, to the student. Evaluation helps them to know where they stand. It helps motivate, direct and integrate learning. A few definitions of fieldwork evaluation are as follows:

- The University of Delhi has outlined the meaning of evaluation of fieldwork training in social work education during the workshop organised by them. "Fieldwork evaluation is a continuous and realistic assessment of a student in terms of his efforts, abilities, work done, learning, use of guidance, personal and professional growth in a particular situation of the field. This is periodically conveyed to the students with an educational objective and which ultimately is instrumental in the award of marks or grades for his overall performance in fieldwork."
- "Evaluation is a process to help the students to realise their abilities and promote them, and also to realise their limitations and to overcome them."
- "Evaluation in fieldwork is defined as the objective appraisal of the workers' total functioning on the job over a specified period of time." –Schmidt and Perry
- "Evaluation is a process which guides and enables students and faculty to evaluate performances on various aspects of the learning process and helps both, as a tool to measure expected learning levels to that of achieved levels of learning. It also helps in identifying strengths to strengthen them, and weaknesses to overcome them." –Iqbal Subhedar

Objectives of Fieldwork Evaluation

The main objectives of fieldwork evaluation in social work education especially of first year students are as follows:

- To assess their knowledge of theory and practicals, and their understanding of the fields of social work.
- To assess the individual abilities of the students to integrate theory and practice in the field.
- To assess the abilities of the students about the application of scientific methods of social work.
- To assess the abilities of the students in writing various

records like diaries, reports and journals.

- To assess the utilisation of social work supervision and guidance by the students during the fieldwork.
- To assess the abilities of the students to prepare a plan of fieldwork or programme and implement it.
- To assess the increase in personal and professional development of the students as a result of professional training imparted to them by experts.

Patterns of Fieldwork Evaluation

The assessment of the performance of students in fieldwork training is normally done by the concerned faculty supervisors under the moderation of the Head of the Department. However, evaluation patterns in practice have their own pros and cons. So far, no pattern has a standard, unbiased method of evaluation. The common patterns of evaluation of fieldwork in social work education in Indian schools of social work are as under:

(i) The concerned faculty supervisor alone evaluates the performance of the students.

(ii) The concerned supervisor and the other faculty members of the schools evaluate and give marks to the students.

(iii) The faculty supervisor evaluates the students under the guidance of the Head of the Department.

(iv) The faculty supervisor makes the main evaluation. This is followed by a viva-voce test in which other faculty members also participate and evaluate.

(v) The faculty supervisor evaluates the performance, as an internal and external, with or without viva-voce.

(vi) The faculty supervisor, as well as the Head of the Department avoid the involvement of agency supervisors in the evaluation process.

(vii) The faculty supervisors/fieldwork coordinators do not conduct any written test along with viva-voce to evaluate the performance of the students on fieldwork.

Process of Fieldwork Evaluation

The process of fieldwork evaluation begins with the placement of students for fieldwork. The evaluation of their performance in the field is done through supervisory meetings and periodical evaluations. The assessment procedure should never come as a surprise to the students and they must be informed in advance that their assessments would be carried out. The assessment should not be a mere formality, it must be taken seriously by both the student and the supervisor. During and after the periodic assessments, students should be appraised of their performances. This would help them to assess their positions in terms of expected norms of achievement vis-a-vis their achievements so far, and on this basis, to better their performances before the next supervisory evaluation session. The final assessment should be unbiased. This is only possible when a committee of the university is constituted and a well-devised format of evaluation is implemented. Evaluation done by the bench is always better, provided it is done systematically, i.e., annual written tests conducted, verification of records done and viva-voce conducted by the university.

The faculty development workshop on fieldwork training organised by the Delhi School of Social Work has recommended a moderation committee for fieldwork evaluation. The committee to be constituted for the purpose should include:

- Two external examiners,
- Head of the Department,
- Fieldwork Coordinator, and
- Concerned Faculty Supervisor.

To evaluate students properly some schools have prepared and implemented standard evaluation sheets. However, these sheets only help the supervisors and the schools to concentrate on the specific areas in which the students have undergone training. A model evaluation sheet of the University of New Castle is given here:

Model of Evaluation Chart

Identification

(i) Name of the student :

(ii) Name of the agency :

(iii) Name of the supervisor :

(iv) Period : From _____ To _____

(v) Number of weeks at three days a week :

(vi) Number of weeks at five days a week :
(vii) Hours per day :

Learning Opportunities

(i) Casework
- (a) Type of client :
- (b) Problem :
- (c) Casework service :

(ii) Administrative procedures
- (a) Case conferences :
- (b) Case presentations :
- (c) Committee meetings :
- (d) Word rounds :
- (e) Opportunity for interdisciplinary and inter-agency discussion and treatment :

Report of Findings in Relation to Performance

(i) Administrative aspects of schools

Agency-related
- (a) Capacity to work within agency function and structure :
- (b) Knowledge of agency function and structure :
- (c) Ability to use administrative procedures constructively :
- (d) Quality of relationships developed with various staff within the agency :

Community-related
- (a) Capacity to work within the community :
- (b) Knowledge of other agencies and resources :
- (c) Relationships with others in the community :

(ii) Recording

Process Records

(a) Do they contain the information necessary, both for the purpose of the agency's service to clients and for the facilitation of teaching and learning? :

(b) How much of the students diagnostic thinking and comments are included, i.e., purpose of interview, situation as student sees it, evaluation comments, plans for next stage? :

(c) Are records up-to-date and given to the supervisor in time to prepare for supervisory session? :

Departmental Records

(a) Are they appreciative of the requirements of the agency? :

(b) Do they convey consciously a picture of the process, a statement of the social work test (related to the agency function) and client's understanding of the situation? :

(c) Are they on time, up-to-date and easy to read? :

(d) Are they used as a tool in pictures? :

Letters and Referrals

(a) Is the content related to the purpose and appropriate to the person addressed? :

(b) Ability to use the English language in all aspects of recording? :

(iii) Use of fieldwork supervision
- (a) To improve student's practice and through this agency's service to clients :
- (b) To facilitate and accelerate student's learning by giving the opportunity to exchange knowledge and ideas arising from the illumination of theory by practice and vice-versa :
- (c) How has the student participated in achieving this purpose? :

(iv) Knowledge and skills in the study (diagnosis-treatment process)

Direct Treatment
- (a) Capacity to make and sustain professional relationships with the clients :
- (b) Capacity to interview purposefully and in a way suited to the particular client :
- (c) Capacity to obtain the necessary information, reflect on it, make a social diagnosis and formulate an appropriate treatment plan :
- (d) Capacity to use a variety of treatment methods appropriately :
- (e) Capacity to modify or all of the above in the light of further information and reflection :
- (f) Interest in understanding psychological, social, cultural factors :

Indirect Treatment

Indirect treatment encompasses those measures used to involve other people either professional or otherwise, who can provide services, effect changes, in their environment in furthering of treatment goals for the client. The range of contacts is wide and the balance will vary with the setting, i.e., as between inter and intra-agency co-operation with social workers, members of other professions and other interested people. :

Development as a Professional Person

This is the sum total of the knowledge and skills described above as acquired and used by each student in the furthering of his education, his agency's services and the welfare of his clients. :

Model Evaluation Sheet of Delhi University

(1) Name of the student :
(2) Name of the agency :
(3) Duration of placement :
(4) Year of study :
(5) Agency supervisor :
(6) Designation :
(7) Faculty supervisor :
(8) Designation :

Content

(1)	Knowledge and understanding of the field	:
(2)	Interaction with the field	:
(3)	Identification of specific areas, needs/resources	:
(4)	Planning, involvement and interaction	:
(5)	Supervisory inputs and its use	:
(6)	Relationship of theory and practice	:
(7)	Recording	:
(8)	Professional development	:
Remarks of the Agency Supervisor		:
Remarks of the Faculty Supervisor		:

Signature (Agency Supervisor) | Signature (Faculty Supervisor)

Need of Method-wise or Programme-wise Evaluation Format

The model formats devised by Delhi University and University of New Castle, UK, for evaluation of performance of the students are inadequate and incomplete as they do not have method-wise or programme-wise evaluation. For proper evaluation formats are required to be devised according to the methods of training for direct techniques, i.e., (i) case work (ii) group work, and (iii) community organisation and other indirect techniques like: (i) social welfare administration, (ii) social work research, and (iii) social action. Formats are also required for programme-wise techniques i.e. (i) camp (ii) study tour (iii) fieldwork through crisis situation, iv) social programmes and movements, (v) films, etc., and source-wise like library, newspapers, magazines, radio, television and personal experiences, etc. The following models or formats of evaluation sheets, devised by the author will be useful and sufficient to evaluate the fieldwork performance of the students and take care of the above-cited shortcomings.

Casework Evaluation Format Model

Personal Data

(1) Name of the student :
(2) Name of the school :
(3) Batch number :
(4) Roll number :
(5) Name of the agency/community :
(6) Name of the faculty supervisor :
(7) Name of the agency supervisor :
(8) Number of visits paid to the agency/community during the academic year :
(9) Number of extra visits paid to the agency with reasons :
(10) Number of cases handled during the year :

Preliminary Preparation

(1) Number of textbooks, reference books, magazines studied before proceeding to the agency and during the process; give name and summary in two lines.
(2) Your views of the literature and comparative analysis of theory and facts, in brief
(3) Observation of phenomena, interaction with inmates or clients, and professional discussions with the faculty and agency supervisors, regarding casework in general and casework process in particular

Background of Casework Practice

(1) Type of cases :
(2) Nature of problems :
(3) Casework services :

Casework Guidance and Field Instruction

(1) Number of individual conferences attended and their use in practice :
(2) Number of group conferences attended and their use in practice :
(3) Utility of guidance/supervision of faculty and agency supervisors in handling the cases and development of the professional skills :
(4) Guidance sought from the interdiscipline experts and its utility :

Use of Casework Principles and Social Work Philosophy

(1) Whether casework principles are used while handling the cases? :
(2) Which principles are being practised? :
(3) Narrate the procedures, methods and situations in which the casework principles are used. :

Preparation of Fieldwork Records

(1) Whether the students have achieved the skills of preparing different kinds of records needed by the agency and the schools and for self-learning :

(2) Whether the records are up-to-date and submitted from time to time for checking :

(3) Whether any innovative style of preparing records is observed :

(4) Whether ability of using appropriate language and administrative approach is developed :

Learning in Practical Situations and Grasping Power

(1) Student's initiative, approach, perspective, etc., with analytical explanations in brief :

(2) Whether the students could develop their social attitudes in the process :

(3) Understanding of the situation and use of intelligence :

(4) Whether grasping power is sharp and able to learn from the field :

Diagnosis and Treatment for Solution of the Problems

(1) Whether the students are able to understand the process of diagnosis :

(2) Whether the students have developed ability to prepare perfect treatment plan :

(3) Whether the students have developed their ability to evaluate their own casework :

(4) Whether follow-up process is practised :

Use of Student's Services to the Agency and School for Social Work Practice

(1) Whether the students are of use to the agency in terms of planning, execution and administration :

(2) Remarks of the agency supervisor, if any :

(3) Whether agency could achieve its goals due to the services of the students :

(4) Whether agency could save any money due to student's services :

(5) Whether students are able to establish relationship with the agency :

(6) Whether students are able to get recognition of the school in the agency and community :

Signature
(Fieldwork Coordinator)

Marks for Casework

Signature
(Director)

Signature
(Coordinator)

Sample of Group Work Evaluation Sheet

Personal Data

(1) Name of the student :

(2) Name of the school :

(3) Batch number :

(4) Roll number :

(5) Name of the agency/community :

(6) Name of the faculty supervisor :

(7) Name of the agency supervisor :

(8) Number of visits paid to the agency/community during the academic year :

(9) Number of extra visits paid to the agency with reasons :

(10) Number of cases handled during the year :

Preliminary Preparation

(1) Number of textbooks, reference books, professional magazines studied before proceeding to the agency, give names and gist in two lines

(2) Views of the literature and comparative analysis of theory and facts in the community

(3) Observation of phenomena, interaction with the agency personnel, group members, faculty supervisors in general and group workers in particulars

Background of Group Work Agency and Group

(1) Background study of the agency and understanding of the students with analytical explanations in brief

(2) Background study of the group members with analytical explanations in brief

(3) Observation of the students regarding attitudes, likes, dislikes, interests, hobbies and

habits of the group members in brief

(4) Nature of the problems and cases pointed out from the group process and handled during the group work

(5) Nature of services rendered to the group members by the group work students

Group Work Guidance and Field Instructions

(1) Number of individual conferences attended and their use in practice

(2) Number of group conferences attended and their use in practice

(3) Utility of the guidance of the faculty and the agency supervisors for group work practice and development of the professional skills

(4) Guidance sought from the experts of other disciplines and its utility for group work practice and professional development

Use of Group Work Principles and Social Work Philosophy

(1) Whether the group work principles are used while practising group work?

(2) Which are the principles practised and the method of practice with analytical explanations in brief?

(3) Are innovative ideas used to implement the principles, with explanation in brief?

Preparation of Fieldwork Records

(1) Whether the students have achieved the skills of preparing different kinds of records needed by the agency the schools, and for their own selves

(2) Whether the records are up-to-date and submitted to the supervisors from time to time for checking and evaluation

(3) Whether any innovative style of preparing the records is made

(4) Ability to use appropriate language

Learning in Practical Situations and Grasping Power

(1) Student's initiative, zeal, approach, sincerity, perspective, etc., observed by the faculty and the agency supervisor be recorded with analytical explanations

(2) Whether the students could develop their positive social attitudes in the process

(3) Understanding of the students about the situations in the field and use of their intelligence or common sense and professional skills for appropriate handling

(4) Whether grasping power of the students is sharp and whether he is able to learn on the field

Diagnosis and Treatment for Solution of the Problems

(1) Whether the students are able to understand the process of diagnosis of group problem and the problems of the members?

(2) Whether the group work students are able to help the group members to develop their social attitudes like co-operation, outlook, character etc.?

(3) Whether the students could inculcate the cultural and moral values in the personality of the group members?

(4) Whether the students could instil self-confidence in the group members to handle any crisis?

(5) Whether the students are able to understand the impact of group work programmes on the group members?

(6) Whether the students observed the problems of the group members and rendered casework services to help them solve their problems?

(7) Whether the students observed any bad habits among the group members and prepared a treatment plan?

(8) Whether the students have developed the ability to evaluate their own group work practice?

(9) Whether the follow-up practice is observed by the students, its impact on the group members, agencies and others?

Use of Students Services to the Agency for Social Welfare Administration and Practice

(1) Whether the students are of use to the schools in terms of planning, execution, administration, etc.?
(2) Observation and remarks of the agency
(3) Whether the agency could achieve the goals through scientific services of the students?
(4) Whether the students are able to establish relations with the agency?
(5) Whether the students could render services to the families of the group members for the development of their personalities and whether they get the recognition of the community?

Signature
(Faculty Supervisor)

Remarks and Marks

Signature
(Director)

Signature
(Coordinator)

Model of Community Organisation Evaluation Sheet

Personal Information

(1) Name of the school :
(2) Name of the student :

(3) Batch number :
(4) Roll number :
(5) Name of the agency/ community :
(6) Name of the faculty supervisor :
(7) Name of the agency supervisor, if any :
(8) Number of visits paid to the agency/field during the academic year :
(9) Number of extra visits paid to the agency/field, with reasons :
(10) Number of cases handled from group work process during the year :

Preliminary Preparation

(1) Number of textbooks, reference books, professional magazines studied before proceeding to the community for practical work with names and gist in brief
(2) Analysis of theory in the books and facts in the society
(3) Observation of the community living, interaction with the people, leaders, social workers and concerned persons
(4) Observation of the work of different social institutions, social agencies, and individual services rendered in the community

Information Regarding Community Setting

(1) Sociological background study of the selected community

(2) Survey, analysis and identification of the problems and needs of the community by the student
(3) Formulation of policy for community development and student's participation and contribution
(4) Programme planning, and student's participation and contribution
(5) Skills of the student in involving the community in planning and policy framing
(6) Identification and mobilisation of local resources
(7) Skills of the students in seeking cooperation of the people living in the community
(8) Nature of the cases and problems pointed out by the students and the expertise services rendered

Guidance of Faculty Supervisors for Community Organisation

(1) Number of individual conferences attended during the academic year and their use in practice
(2) Number of group conferences attended during the academic year and their use in practice
(3) Whether guidance sought from the experts of different discipline; their use in practice
(4) Whether the students could develop their knowledge regarding the procedure and

practice of social work due to supervision of the supervisors

Use of Principles of Community Organisation

(1) Whether the students have used the principles of community organisation in practice
(2) Which principles are used? State procedures and methods in brief
(3) Any innovative ideas used to implement the principles of community organisation and philosophy of social work
(4) Practical difficulties in implementing the principles, and the skills used to overcome them
(5) Programme implementation and participation of the people
(6) Community work done with integrated approach and student's understanding in this regard

Preparation of Fieldwork Records

(1) Whether the students could skillfully prepare their records for the schools and the community, and for themselves
(2) Whether the records are up-to-date and are submitted to the supervisors from time to time for checking and evaluation

(3) Whether the students have used any innovative style of preparing records
(4) Ability of using appropriate language

Learning in Practical Situations and Grasping Power

(1) Whether the students had zeal, interest, initiative, sincerity, and social perspective while learning in practical situations
(2) Whether the students have gained sufficient field knowledge
(3) Whether the students have learnt the use of social work techniques and skills in the field
(4) Whether students have learnt communication skills, interaction and observation methods practically
(5) Whether the students have developed their positive social attitudes in the process
(6) Understanding of the students about the practical situations in the field and use of their intelligence and common sense with professional skills for appropriate handling of situations
(7) Ability to learn fast
(8) Whether the professional approach is developed

Diagnosis and Treatment

(1) Whether the students are able to understand the process of diagnosis of community problem

(2) Whether the students could create an awareness among the people to develop their social attitudes

(3) Whether the students with the help of the supervisors and the schools fulfil the needs of the community

(4) Which social work techniques are used to help the people in the community

(5) Whether the students could inculcate the cultural and moral values in the personality of the people

(6) Whether the students could develop the self-confidence of the people to solve their problems

(7) Nature of the services provided to the people in the community

(8) Whether the students could solve the problems of the community

(9) Whether the students have developed the ability to evaluate their own community work

(10) Whether follow-up practice is observed by the students

Use of Students' Services for Social Work Practice

(1) Whether the students were of use to the community and the schools in terms of planning, execution and administration
(2) Whether the community could be organised well
(3) Whether the students could establish professional relations with the community
(4) General observations

Signature
(Faculty Supervisor)

Remarks and Marks

Signature
(Director)

Signature
(Coordinator)

Social Welfare Administration Work Evaluation Sheet: Model

Personal Data

(1) Name of the school :
(2) Name of the student :
(3) Batch number :
(4) Roll number :
(5) Name of the agency/community :
(6) Name of the faculty supervisor :
(7) Name of the agency supervisor :
(8) Number of visits paid to the agency/community during the year :
(9) Number of extra visits paid during the year :

Preliminary Preparation

(1) Number of textbooks, reference books, professional magazines studied before proceeding to the agency/community with names and gist in two lines.

(2) Discussions and analysis of the matter

Background of Agency/Community

(1) Background study of the agency/community

(2) Student's abilities and administrative qualities in bringing together people of different philosophies, political affiliations, approaches and thinking for a common cause

Guidance and Field Instructions

(1) Guidance sought from the faculty supervisors for organising meets

(2) Guidance sought from the agency supervisors for administering programmes

(3) Guidance sought from experts, if any, for organising, administering programmes

(4) Use of guidance, instructions of social welfare administration for developmental programme

Use of Social Work Philosophy and Principles of Social Welfare Administration

(1) Whether the philosophy and principles of social welfare administration are used for practising SWA
(2) Specify the philosophy and principles used for practice
(3) Any new idea used for implementing the philosophy and principles

Preparation of Fieldwork Records

(1) Quantity of records prepared
(2) Whether records of SWA are up-to-date and are submitted to the faculty supervisors on time
(3) Whether any innovative style of preparing the records is observed
(4) Is the language correct and up to the mark

Learning and Grasping Power in Practical Situations

(1) Student's initiative, zeal, approach, sincerity, perspective, etc., observed by the faculty and the agency supervisors
(2) Whether the students could develop a positive social attitude towards the people/community and the administration of social welfare schemes?
(3) Are the students professionally capable of

handling different personalities, groups, sub-groups and communities in terms of organisation and social welfare administration

(4) Whether grasping power of the students is sharp and are they able to learn fast on the field

Solution of the Problem

(1) Whether the students are able to develop the social attitudes like cooperation, outlook, character, etc.

(2) Whether the students could teach good cultural and moral values to the people during the practice of welfare measures

(3) Handling of difficult social situation, especially where differences of opinion exist

(4) Did the students impart to the villagers the philosophy of unity and solidarity

(5) Whether the students could make the people think scientifically about the community organisations, community development and its administration?

Social Welfare Administrative Practice in Fieldwork Students

(1) Whether the students are of use to the agency/community in terms of planning, organising, executing and administering of welfare measures/programmes/project

(2) Observation of social attitudes and tendencies of people in terms of SWA
(3) Whether the agency/community could achieve the goals due to SWA of the students and their scientific services
(4) Whether the students could render services to the agency/community for making them aware of their needs, problems, etc.
(5) Whether the students are able to establish relations with the community leaders, etc.

Signature (Faculty Supervisor) Signature (Student)

Research Work Evaluation Sheet: Example

Personal Data

(1) Name of the school :
(2) Name of the student :
(3) Batch number :
(4) Roll number :
(5) Name of the agency/community :
(6) Name of the faculty supervisor :
(7) Name of the agency supervisor :
(8) Number of visits paid to the agency/community during the year :
(9) Number of extra visits paid during the year :

Preliminary Preparation

(1) Number of textbooks, reference books, professional magazines studied before proceeding to the agency/community with names and gist in two lines

(2) Discussions and analysis of the theoretical information and facts and practices before proceeding to the agency/community

Background of Agency/Community

(1) Background study of the agency/community and understanding of the agency services, beneficiaries/community people with analytical explanations in brief

(2) Identifying the needs and problems of the agencies, beneficiaries, community, people, etc., and use of social work research technique for solving these problems

Guidance and Field Instructions

(1) Guidance sought from the faculty supervisors for making use of SWR technique

(2) Guidance sought from the agency supervisors in making use of SWR technique

(3) Guidance sought from experts, if any, for making use of SWR technique

Use of Theory and Method of Social Work Research

(1) Whether the theory and methods of SWR are used for social work practice

(2) Any new idea is used for implementing theory and methods of SWR for social work practice

(3) Whether answers of practical questions faced by the social work practitioners are found through SWR technique

(4) Whether social work research technique is useful in solving complicated field problems

Preparation of Fieldwork Records

(1) Whether the students have achieved the skills of preparing different kinds of records

(2) Whether records of SWR are up-to-date and submitted to the faculty supervisors on time for checking and evaluation

(3) Whether any innovative style of preparing the records is observed

(4) Whether appropriate language is used

Learning and Grasping Power in Practical Situations

(1) Whether students could understand the need of making use of social work research in the field for getting solutions to complicated problems

(2) Understanding of the students about situations in the field and use of their intelligence and professional skills for making use of SWR
(3) Whether grasping power of the students is sharp

Solution of the Problem

(1) Whether the students are well trained in making use of SWR for getting solutions to practical problems
(2) Whether the students could make the people/agency/ community realise the significance of SWR for scientific social work practice

Use of Social Work Research Technique to the Agency/Community

(1) Whether the students are of use to the agency/community in terms of using SWR technique and social work practice
(2) Whether the students are able to establish relations with the people/community leaders, etc.

Signature (Faculty Supervisor)	Signature (Student)

Social Action Evaluation Sheet: Sample

Personal Data

(1) Name of the school :
(2) Name of the student :

(3) Batch number :
(4) Roll number :
(5) Name of the agency/community :
(6) Name of the faculty supervisor :
(7) Name of the agency supervisor :
(8) Number of visits paid to the agency/community during the year :
(9) Number of extra visits paid during the year :

Preliminary Preparation

(1) Number of textbooks, reference books, professional magazines studied before proceeding to the agency/community with names and gist in two lines
(2) Discussions and analysis of the theoretical information/knowledge and facts and practices before proceeding to the agency/community

Background of Agency/Community

(1) Background study of the agency/community and understanding of the agency services, beneficiaries/ community people
(2) Identifying the needs and problems of the agencies, beneficiaries, community, people, etc., and use of social work research technique for understanding the nature of problems

Guidance and Field Instructions

(1) Guidance sought from the faculty supervisors for making use of SA technique

(2) Guidance sought from the agency supervisors making use of SA technique

(3) Guidance sought from experts, if any, for making use of SA technique

(4) Use of guidance, instructions of social action for the developmental programme

Use of Social Work Philosophy and Principles of Social Action

(1) Whether the theory and methods of SA are used for social work practice

(2) Any new idea is used for implementing theory and methods of SA for social work practice

(3) Whether answers practical questions faced by the social work practitioners are found through SA technique

(4) Whether social action technique is useful in solving complicated field problem.

Preparation of Fieldwork Records

(1) Whether the students have achieved the skills of preparing different kinds of records

(2) Whether records of SWR are up-to-date and submitted to the faculty supervisors time to time for checking and evaluation

(3) Whether any innovative style of preparing the records is observed
(4) Ability of using appropriate language

Learning in Practical Situations and Grasping Power

(1) Student's initiative, zeal, approach, sincerity, perspective, etc., observed by the faculty and the agency supervisors
(2) Whether the students could develop their positive social attitudes towards the organisation of people/community and the administration of social welfare schemes
(3) Understanding of the students about the situation in the field and use of their intelligence and professional skills for handling different personalities, groups, sub-groups and community in terms of organisation and social welfare administration
(4) Whether grasping power of the students is sharp

Solving the Problem

(1) Whether the students are able to understand the process of making use of social action to comprehend the nature, scope, extension and magnitude of social problems

(2) Whether the students used different methods like rallies, street plays, exhibition of posters, competitions, in mobilising opinion of people against the social evil
(3) Whether the students used the principles and philosophies of social work for making people realise the social problems
(4) Whether the students could create awareness among the people about the need of effective solutions to avoid recurrence of such problem.
(5) Whether students neglected use of social action for solving problems.

Use of Social Action Technique to the Agency/Community

(1) Whether the students are of use to the agency/community in terms of planning, organising, executing and administering of welfare measures/programmes/project
(2) Observation of social attitudes and tendencies of people/community in terms of SWA
(3) Whether the agency/community could achieve the goals through SWA of the students and their scientific services.
(4) Whether the students could render services to the agency/community for making them aware of their needs, problems, etc.

(5) Whether the students are able to establish relations with the people/community leaders, etc.

Signature (Faculty Supervisor) Signature (Student)

Model: Study Tour Evaluation Sheet

(1) Name :
(2) Batch number :
(3) Roll number :
(4) Name of the faculty supervisor :
(5) Tour area and duration :
(6) Present or absent :
(7) Reasons for absence :
(8) Tour schedule :
(9) Participation in learning :
(10) Participation in discussions :
(11) Participation in organising :
(12) Participation in recreation :
(13) Group behaviour :
(14) Exemplary services rendered :
(15) Practical knowledge gained during the tour :
(16) Whether students were useful to the school during organising :
(17) Participated in seminar on study tour :
(18) Submission of report :
(19) Marks deserved by the student :

Signature Signature

Model: Camp Work Evaluation Sheet

(1) Name of the student :
(2) Year and batch number :
(3) Area of camp :
(4) Roll number :

(5) Name of the faculty supervisor :

(6) Number of days of camp :

(7) Duration of the camp :

(8) Present days/Absent days :

(9) Reason of absenteeism :

(10) Activities in which contributed services : Organisation/ Planning/Guidance/ Counselling

(11) Activities in which he/she did not take interest and reasons for the same :

(12) Methods and skills used for social service and social work :

(13) Total days of halt made and total hours worked :

(14) Exemplary work done in the camp by the student :

(15) Opinions and suggestions of the students regarding camp in general :

(16) Marks deserved by the student :

Signature
(Camp Coordinator)

Signature
(Student)

Think and Do

"Make an attempt to overcome your social weaknesses and convert them into building a career in social work."

Chapter 12

Summer Training

"Practical training imparted during the summer on how to set up voluntary organisations can give the students the confidence in helping them set up their own voluntary organisations for professional social work practice."

Introduction

In the last six and half decades of social work education in India, the schools of social work have been imparting training to the students of MSW first year, in two phases in a traditional manner: (1) orientation training, and (2) concurrent fieldwork training. During the first phase of training, the students are taken to different social welfare agencies situated in local areas as well as to the agencies located outside their areas for introductory observational studies of voluntary organisations, and their practices of using social work techniques and skills. This training is completed in one or two months. In the second phase, the students are placed in the same social welfare agencies for concurrent fieldwork training throughout the academic year to learn from the concerned persons about working with individuals, groups and communities. This training is completed in one year.

In fact, the fieldwork training in social work education was devised in America and it is practised in India as it is since 1936 with only a few changes in its nature and scope. Trained professional scholars have conducted experiments and researches on fieldwork training and have tried to analyse it critically. Schools and the universities have also organised number of seminars and workshops and reported their observations in national and international magazines with viable suggestions for improvement.

Accordingly changes have been made in terms of number of

visits, number of programmes, their nature, scope, extent and magnitude, but keeping the existing system in tact. However, in all these years, in India, neither the schools of social work nor the associations of trained professional social workers of different states, have given thought to the shortcomings of the training system, and the needs of the Indian people and organisations. Due to this the students of MSW Part I are deprived of certain need-based essentials or foundation training which are very important in professional courses.

Taking into consideration the limitations of the existing system of fieldwork training and the need for its extension and expansion, an attempt has been made by the author to introduce a third phase in the training procedure, namely, summer training. This phase trains the students and gives them an insight into the methods of setting up and developing voluntary organisations for creating self-employment as also employment for others. The said training programme can be scheduled during the summer vacations after the annual examination of the first year. All the students should compulsorily be made to undergo this training under the faculty supervisors and professionally trained people. To make the schools, teachers, supervisors, and the students understand the nature, scope, extent and magnitude of this training, the author has framed the objectives of summer training.

Objectives of Summer Training

- To provide an opportunity to the students to study the official procedure of registering voluntary organisations.
- To understand the infrastructure required for setting up voluntary organisations.
- To make use of expert services available in the society for setting up voluntary organisations.
- To make the students aware of the community resources which may then be utilised for setting up voluntary services.
- To provide an opportunity to the students to prepare the required official papers, on the basis of needs and schemes available, for registration of the voluntary organisations.
- To make the students prepare programmes according to the objectives and goals formed by the workers while setting up voluntary organisations.

- To enable the students utilise community resources to raise required funds and manpower to implement the programmes chalked out by the workers.
- To introduce the students to local, state, national and international funding agencies, thereby making them aware of the procedures for getting funds, terms and conditions for developing voluntary organisations, etc.
- To help the students understand the entire procedure of setting up NGOs, using resources, getting funds and procedure of utilising the funds, preparing programmes, implementing them for the welfare of the people, creating employment for self-support and for others and the scope for professional practices instead of running after jobs/services.
- To make the students understand the ways of using their learning and training for their own support, to help the needy and people with problems to help themselves and to get social recognition to the profession by widening its scope.

Summer Training Curriculum

The objectives mentioned above shed light on the significance of summer training and its need for widening the scope for setting up independent professional practices instead of simply producing trained manpower and making them look for elusive jobs. To make the students stand on their own, after undergoing a professional concurrent training, is the main objective of summer camps. A systematic summer training curriculum has to be devised, to make the summer training meaningful, useful and worthy. The author has made an attempt to frame a specific practical-oriented curricula which is as under:

- Registering a voluntary organisation and paper work involved, relating to obtaining the registration certificate, formats, correspondence, fees, papers, files, etc.
- Defining office procedures and functions of the voluntary organisations to achieve its goals.
- Methods and ways of devising welfare programmes in accordance with the objectives and goals, procedures and functions.
- Preparing fund-raising programme proposals with estimates, plan and procedure of implementation.

- Utilising available resources, i.e., man, material, money for work.
- Identifying the needs of the community by conducting surveys, conferences, informal meets, door-to-door visits and set the need-based goals.
- Collecting the addresses of the local, state level, national and international funding agencies, sources, etc.
- Preparing proposals for obtaining funds from different agencies, its procedure and method.
- Collecting information regarding state government and central government schemes.
- Performing professional practices and methods of solving problems of the needy and poor through the agency.

Training and Learning Process

The above curriculum assists the faculty supervisors and outside trainers to impart training about practical aspects of NGOs in real life situations. However, to make use of time, money, labour, and energy properly, different learning methods should be used to make the training and learning process effective and useful for the purpose of achieving the goals or making the summer courses meaningful. Theoretically speaking the curriculum looks very simple and easy but practically it is tough, difficult and complicated. Therefore, the following processes need to be followed by the students:

(i) Theoretical participation under the guidance of supervisors,
(ii) Discussion with the faculty supervisors and external trainers,
(iii) Careful preparations,
(iv) Visiting the concerned offices to learn different procedures, and
(v) Preparing a sketch of the entire training.

The following literature will also be useful to the students:

- Voluntary Organisations in India
- The Society Registration Act, 1860
- State Government Rules framed under the SR Act, 1860
- The Public Trust Act, 1952
- State Government rules formed under the PT Act, 1952
- Funding Agencies in India and Abroad
- Compendium of Central Government Schemes for NGOs

- Compendium of State Government Schemes for NGOs
- Fund Raising Proposal Formats
- Programme Charts Formats
- Model Constitution of NGOs
- Registers, Forms, Proceedings, etc.

Setting up an NGO

Students of social work are "would-be professional practitioners". They must know the existing procedures of registration of NGOs, for setting up their own NGOs as well as to guide people in setting up an NGOs with a view to fulfilling their needs. To guide people on this is a tough task from the technical, legal and social point of view. Legal and technical advisors are easily available, but there is a dearth of social advisors. Therefore, students must be conscious enough to learn this aspect under the guidance of the faculty supervisors. Since the social aspect of establishing NGOs, is gaining political overtones, one must be careful to see that the organisation is not taken over by political activists after all the efforts of establishing, getting grants and earning goodwill has been done. Caution should be exercised especially in the following areas:

- Selection of people (staff),
- Selection of the field,
- Selection of the area of operation, and
- Selection of the programmes.

Selection of the Staff

According to the existing laws, seven members can come together to form a body of the organisation. Of these three members will have to be chosen as executives, i.e., (i) The President, (ii) The Secretary, and (iii) The Treasurer, and the remaining will be Directors. Theoretically and legally, there is no compulsion of choosing people belonging to a particular religion or caste group to form this voluntary organisation. However, practically it is suggested that the members must represent as many religions/caste groups as possible to make the organisation more cosmopolitan in nature and thereby create a socially positive image. Like-minded people having good nature, character, perspectives, zeal for constructive work, interest for social work, loyalty to the leader and the organisation, should be selected. However, their honesty, sense of gratitude, social attitudes and positive thinking, social approaches, selfishness, usefulness in terms of resourcefulness, etc., must be judged on the basis of the leader's experience and observations and examination of the information collected from others. Decisions taken relating to the selection of the office bearers at this initial stage is very important because the success of the NGO depends upon the selection of the right people. So the founder should be aware of the principles of selection of the right men for the right job.

Selection of the Field

There are various fields of social services but selection of the field or fields depends upon the knowledge, social perspectives and experiences of the founder. In general it has been seen that the founders are either politically motivated people or politicians themselves. They choose a field, which will enhances their political image in society.

Ideally the founder has to consider his interests, in addition to identifying the needs of the region before the field of social service is chosen. Political motivations or availability of government grants must not be the deciding factors. It is said that the founder should think of developing the NGOs with a sense of benefiting to the concerned people rather than thinking of his own gains or governmental facilities. However, this is easier said than done. Taking this into consideration the founder should study various governmental/non-governmental, Indian and foreign schemes of social work, the funds available for them and identify the needs of the people or communities/places/pockets where the services will be rendered and only then the field/s should be chosen.

Selection of the Area of Operation

The choice of the area of operation of the proposed organisation depends on the founders. Normally the area selected is the political constituency guided more by a selfish motto. The area of operation should be chosen considering the needs of the people. It is ultimately the deprived, the needy and the suffering who are the beneficiaries of the services. Hence, remote areas should be kept in mind to extend the services in future. However, initially one has to think of familiar regions because resources must be mobilised till it earns the goodwill of the society. Once this is done, the founder need not bother about funds and resources because these will automatically pour in from different sections of the society.

Selection of the Programmes

Programmes are normally selected by NGOs considering the possibility of getting funds from different sources in the society. Programmes should be chalked out considering their utility in terms of social change and social development for the people of the region. Societal and national problems should be given importance and the dire needs of the areas must be given priority. To render scientific social work services the programmes should be chalked out on the basis of the objectives and the goals of the organisation. Students therefore, should bear in mind that it is the selection of appropriate programmes, which is vital for the success of an NGO. Therefore they should study and analyse for suitability, the programmes of local, regional, state, national and international voluntary organisations, before deciding their own.

Informal Meeting of Probable Directors

The founder of the NGO has to take into consideration traits such as like-mindedness and social orientation of probable candidates for the post of directors of the proposed voluntary organisation before selecting them. To select the right people, a list of names of the probable candidates should be prepared and the candidates judged skillfully regarding suitability. After the selection the founder should collect information about the candidates from different sources and then call them for an informal discussion to seek their consent and also to give them an idea about the formation of the proposed voluntary organisation, its objectives, programmes, short and long term plans, etc. After this stage, a formal meeting of all probable directors should be called for finalising the formation of the organisation. An agenda is sent to them well in advance. The agenda could be as follows:

Agenda

A meeting of the social workers of _______ will be held on __________ at _________ sharp, in the office of the ___________ to transact the following business.

(i) To discuss the formation of the voluntary organisation of social workers of _________ in near future.
(ii) To discuss and finalise the name of the proposed voluntary organisation.
(iii) To discuss and form a body of the proposed voluntary organisation.
(iv) To discuss and authorise one individual to take the initiative to complete the formalities of registration.
(v) To discuss and frame the objectives and goals of the proposed voluntary organisation.
(vi) To discuss the concerned subjects/items placed before the proposed body, i.e., office for registration, office for functions, etc.

Place:
Date:

Sd/-

____

Founder of the proposed organisation

Formal Meeting of the Proposed Board

Members Present Signature

(i)
(ii)
(iii)
(iv)
(v)

A formal meeting of the Board of Directors of the proposed voluntary organisation should be called to complete the process of formation of the body. Discussions must be held according to the agenda and, opinions and suggestions made by the members regarding framing of the objectives and goals, membership fees, donations, programmes, properties, office for registration, office for function, etc., should be recorded. Authorised persons should be nominated for passing resolutions because certain resolutions will have to be attached or enclosed with the papers of registration as well as kept for inspection. The preliminary record is very important from the point of view of the registration, inspection, emergency and crisis management, conflict and dispute, etc., in future.

To prepare a systematic record the founder of the organisation should maintain a Proceedings book. Ready printed Proceedings books are available in the market. The founder should also take care to maintain the receipts of official expenditure, i.e., receipts of purchase of Proceedings book, receipt fees of registration, travel fares, receipts of the fees of advocates if any, printing bills, postal receipts, phone bills, telegram bills, etc. It is important to keep a record of the small expenditures also because they are not only useful accounts but they are valuable evidence during a crisis. The founders should maintain a Proceedings book and record the proceedings as follows:

Proceedings of the Meeting

The proceedings of formal/official meeting of the Board of Directors of the proposed voluntary organisation was held on _________ at _______________.

Mr. _______________, founder/initiator was requested to preside over the chair of the meeting. Considering the request of all the present members he presided over the chair, expressed his thanks to all of them and appealed to the present members to discuss about the formation of the organisation and to extend their cooperation.

Mr. ________________ proposed the name of the initiator/founder for the post of the President of the proposed voluntary organisation and Mr. ______________ seconded. Mr. ______________________ founder accepted the proposal and a resolution was passed by all members.

Mr. __________ proposed the name of Mr. __________ for the post of the Secretary and Mr. __________ seconded it. Mr. ___________ accepted the responsibility and a resolution was passed by all the members.

Mr. ___________ proposed the name of Mr. __________ for the post of the Jt. Secretary and Mr. ___________ seconded it. Mr. _______________ accepted the proposal and agreed to function as Jt. Secretary and a resolution was passed by all the members.

Mr. ___________ proposed the name of Mr. _________ for the post of the Treasurer and Mr. ________ seconded it. Mr. _________ accepted the offer of the members and a resolution was passed by all the members.

Mr. _________ founder President proposed the names of (i) Mr. _________, (ii) Mr. __________, (iii) Mr. ________, for the posts of the directors and Mr. _________ seconded it and all the three persons agreed to function as Directors.

Mr. __________, founder President, suggested three probable names for the proposed voluntary organisation and all the members accepted all those three names to place before the authority for finalisation and a resolution was passed by all the members.

Mr. __________, founder President, proposed the name of Mr. _________, Secretary of the organisation, to complete the formalities of registration of the organisation and all the members agreed for the same and a resolution was passed by all the members.

Mr. __________ explained his ideas and plans and requested all the members to share their experiences, ideas and plans. Every member participated in the discussion and the following ideas were accepted and the suggestions recorded for forming the objectives, goals, and memorandum constitution of the organisation and the Secretary was asked to prepare the papers in consultation with the experts and approval of the Board or President for registration.

The founder President suggested that for registration the address of his house may be given and all the members agreed for the same and passed a resolution.

The meeting of the Board was over in a free and frank manner with a decision of formation of the organisation and its registration.

Sd	Sd
President	Secretary

Registration Papers

The authorised person of the proposed organisation should prepare the following papers:

(i) Request letter to get exemption from publishing notice in the paper.

(ii) Request letter (covering letter) for registration of the organisation.

(iii) A consent letter from the directors for registration.
(iv) A guarantee letter for proper use of the certificate.
(v) A covering letter to the superintendent mentioning list of papers.
(vi) Rules and Regulations of the organisation.
(vii) Certificate of original rules.
(viii) Schedule to be filled in showing the number of employees.
(ix) The list of the members.
(x) A consent letter addressed to the superintendent with signatures of executives.
(xi) Authorisation letter to the authorised person to make alterations in papers, etc.
(xii) Covering letter to the executive magistrate for affidavit.
(xiii) Affidavit on stamp papers of Rs. 10.

To prepare these papers either an advocate is to be consulted or an expert in the concerned offices. The consultants charge minimum Rs. 1000 (could change from place to place and time) for preparing papers and assisting the founders to get the organisation registered. Moreover, the founders or the students may not understand the procedure and method. Hence details of setting up a voluntary organisations have been provided here.

A specimen copy of the request letter is given hereunder for reference.

Schedule `A'

To,
Hon'ble Assistant Superintendent,
Office of the Charity Commission,
_______________________ Division,
_______________________________.

Subject: Request for Registration of our Trust/Society under the Public Trust Act, 1950, and the Societies Registration Act, 1860.

Sir,
We are submitting herewith the following documents for registration of our Trust/Society i.e. ____________________, under the above mentioned Acts and Rules.

(i) Memorandum of Association,
(ii) Rules and Regulations,
(iii) Consent letter of the Board.
(iv) Letter as regards address of the trust, property, etc., on stamp paper of Rs. 10/- with court fee stamp of Rs.___/-
(v) Letter regarding use of registration certificate.

We also write to inform you that the objectives of our Trust/Society are according to Section 20 of the Societies Registration Act, 1860, and there is no Trust/Society in our village/town with the same name.

We are ready to pay Rs. ___ as the fee for registration of the Trust/Society. You are, therefore, requested to register our Trust at the earliest and oblige.

Thanking you,

Yours sincerely,

Encl: As above.

Schedule `B'

Model: Memorandum of Association

Name of the Society
(1) The Registered Office and Address
(2) Area of Operation/Jurisdiction
The area of operation of the society shall be __________.
(3) Objectives of the Society
The objectives of the society are:
(a) *Educational Services*

- To start *balwadis*, primary schools, residential schools, schools for the physically and mentally handicapped, schools for professional education, vocational education, night schools, industrial training centres/schools, etc., or to take over existing Schools/Institutes.
- To start libraries in rural and urban areas or to take over libraries.
- To provide books, notebooks and educational equipment to the poor, needy and intelligent students.

- To start hostels and boarding facilities for the poor and needy school-going girls and boys.
- To start hostels and boarding for working women and men.
- To provide scholarships, finance, and giving prizes to studious and intelligent students.
- To impart practical training to the women and men, handicapped children, etc., for different jobs, business, etc.
- To conduct adult education classes, social education, and population education classes in rural and urban areas.

(b) *Social Services*:

- To start marriage counselling for widows, divorcees, physically handicapped and girls and boys of all religions and castes.
- To mobilise public opinion against social problems, social evils, bad customs and traditions, superstitions and blind beliefs, and spreading science for the people of rural and urban areas.
- To start family counselling centres for solving marital conflicts, tensions and problems for the betterment of the family, society and nation.
- To participate in the functions and programmes organised by the voluntary organisations, government organisations for social service, social welfare and social reforms.
- To organise different programmes, services for rural and urban development.
- To construct Samaj Mandirs in urban and rural areas.
- To provide funeral benefits and expenses to the poor and the destitute.
- To construct marriage halls for all religions and castes, and also halls for cultural programmes in rural and urban areas.
- To organise mass marriages for different communities and encourage intercaste and interreligious marriages.
- To start old age homes in rural and urban areas.
- To start recreation halls/clubs for aged people, youth, workers, children and women.

- To open research institutes for conducting social researches on different social problems of rural and urban communities.
- To implement the projects of central governments, Central Social Welfare Board, State Social Welfare and other government social welfare schemes.
- To participate in the social reform movement in India.
- To organise social service camps, social health camps, *shramdan*, blood donation camps, eye camps, school health, etc., in rural and urban areas.
- To start crèches for children of workers in rural and urban areas.
- To create awareness among the rural and urban people regarding their social, political, economic, psychological, emotional, personal and domestic problems.
- To set up employees cooperative societies, mahila co-operative societies, cash credit societies, youth development banks, rural cooperative banks, etc.
- To organise child welfare, family welfare, youth welfare, women's welfare, labour welfare programmes in rural and urban areas.
- To open beggar homes and rehabilitation centres for leprosy patients, prostitutes, *devdasis*, unmarried mothers and other girls and boys having problems.
- To organise programmes and film shows for reducing untouchability in rural and urban areas.
- To mobilise people against corruption, gambling, *matka* (*lotteries*), etc.
- To start school social work projects in rural and urban areas.
- To start *muktangans* for rehabilitating alcoholic patients.
- To start *balbhavans* for imparting good *sanskars* (virtues) in children.
- To start labour welfare centres.
- To form society against prevention of crime and for rehabilitation of young offenders, juvenile delinquents and criminals in rural and urban areas.
- To open nature cure centres.
- To start orphan homes in rural and urban areas.

- To start workers' education centres to make them literate.
- To start marginal farmers' welfare centres.
- To form industrial counselling services in rural and urban areas for solving personal, domestic, social and industrial problems of workers.

(c) *Medical Services*:

- Socialisation of medicine, starting nursing homes, hospitals, dispensaries in rural and urban areas for providing free medical treatment to the poor and the needy.
- To organise free medical camps in rural and urban areas.
- To organise family planning camps and creating favourable public opinion in its favour.
- To open blood banks in rural and urban areas.
- To organise camps for social health, community health, competition of good health programmes, eye camps, lectures and workshops for health.
- To start hospital for treatment and rehabilitation of alcoholic patients.

(d) *Recreational Services*:

- To open sports clubs in rural and urban areas.
- To construct grounds/stadia to encourage sports and games, especially among the youth.
- To start gymkhanas.
- To organise for training in sports/games, both indoor and outdoor.
- To purchase sports material, awards, prizes and financial aid to sports persons.
- Organise film shows, dramas, orchestras, etc.

(4) Loss and Profits

The profit and loss, if any, will be utilised only for the purpose of the above objectives.

Schedule `C'

The personal information of the members of the Trust/Society, i.e., ____________________, to whom the power and authority is given under the Constitution of the Trust/Society, for its administration and management are as follows:

Sr. No.	*Full Name and Address*	*Designation*	*Age*	*Nationality*	*Occupation*

Sd/-	Sd/-	Sd/-	Sd/-	Sd/-
President	Vice President	Secretary	Jt. Secretary	Treasurer

Place:
Date:

Schedule `D'

We, the members of ____________________ Trust/Society, hereby declare that we have come together to bring into existence the above mentioned institution under the Public Trust Act, 1952, and the Societies Registration Act, 1860, and rules thereunder. With this intention it is established on _______________ and signed on the statement for the same.

Sr. No.	*Full Name and Address*	*Signature*

Place:
Date:

Signatures of Witnesses
(i)
(ii)

We recognise the above persons and their signatures.

Seal
Executive Magistrate/Advocate.

Model: Rules and Regulations

(1) Definition:

The rules and regulations of the Society are as under:

(a) "SWAD" means Social Workers (Professional) and Social Scientists.

(b) "The Act" means The *(state)* Societies Registration Act, 1960, and amendments thereon.

(c) "The Rules" means The *(state)* Societies Registration Rules, *(year)*, and amendments thereon.

(d) "The Board" means the Board of Directors of the Society.

(e) "The Registrar" means the Registrar appointed under the Act or the Inspector General of Registration in *(state)*.

(f) "The Government" means the Government of *(state)*, the Government of India.

(g) "Society Fund" means the property of the Society, i.e., (i) Money, (ii) Fixed Property–Land and Building, and (iii) Donations.

(h) "Accounting Year" means a period of 12 months beginning 1st April till the 31st of March.

(i) The words and expressions not defined in these bylaws but defined in the Act or the Rules shall have meaning assigned to them in the Act or Rules.

(2) Membership:

The membership of the SWAD Welfare Society shall consist of trained professional Social Workers and Social Scientists of________ and ________ states only.

Eligibility for Membership:

(a) Any trained social worker who has completed Master of Social Work Course from any Indian or Foreign University or Institute and possessing minimum five years experience in rendering social services and who agrees with the rules and regulations of the society, can become a member of the Society provided the Board of Directors agrees to accept him/her as a temporary/permanent/life member of the Society.

(b) Any social scientist who has completed Masters Degree in Social Sciences and the M.Phil. course or Doctorate in Social Sciences from any Indian or Foreign University or

Institute and possessing minimum five years experience in rendering social services and who agrees with the rules and regulations of the society, can become a member of the Society provided the Board of Directors agrees to accept him/her as a temporary/permanent/life member of the Society.

(c) Any person who is a graduate in Social Science or Social Work from any Indian or Foreign University or Institute and possessing minimum ten years experience in professional social work or fifteen years experience voluntary social services and who agrees with the rules and regulations of the Society, can become a member of the society provided the Board of Directors agrees to accept him/her as a temporary/permanent/life member of the Society.

(d) None other than a trained professional social worker or social scientist is eligible to become either temporary or life member of the Society even if he/she is possessing the experience of rendering social services.

Procedure:

(a) Every trained professional social worker or social scientist intending to become a member of the Society shall have to submit an application in writing in the prescribed form and shall have to pay the subscribed amount and an entrance fee of Rs. 10 along with the application, provided that no such application shall be required from the same person for the application for the registration of the Society under the Act.

(b) The Society shall, within three months from the date on which application for admission was delivered to such society, either admit or refuse to admit any such person as a member and shall send a written communication of such acceptance or refusal to the applicant before the said period (without citing any reason of refusal). If no communication of admission as a member is received by the applicant before expiry of the said period, his/her application for admission shall be deemed to have been refused by the society on the last day of the said period. The decision of the Board of Directors regarding acceptance or rejection shall be final.

(c) All the members of the Society will be called Society Members and all of them will be having equal rights, and the decisions taken by the Board of Directors from time to time will be binding on all the members of the Society.

(d) Right of the Members: Any member, who desires to check up the accounts of the Society, has to inform the secretary in writing at least a day before he desires to do so. Moreover, he will have to mention the reason/ purpose and subject matter in his application.

(e) No member should ask for checking the accounts with *mala fide* intentions or just to harass the Board of Directors or member of the Board. The Secretary will have right to accept or reject such applications without assigning any reason for the same.

(3) Termination of Membership:

The Board can remove any such Member of the society from the register of members:

(a) who willfully deceives the Society or furnishes false information or is convicted of any offence or is adjudicated insolvent or intentionally does any act prejudicial to the interest of the society.

(b) who violates the rules and regulations and whose behaviour spoils the image of the Society.

(c) who collects any money/fund from any person/ organisation/government without the knowledge or permission of the Society or Board.

(d) who fails to pay the subscription of the society for a continuous period of three years.

(e) who resigns.

Provided that no member shall be removed from the register unless a reasonable opportunity is given to him to show cause why he should not be removed from the register of members of the Society.

(4) Subscriptions:

(a) All persons eligible to become members of the Society shall have to subscribe Rs. 100 per annum and shall have to pay an entrance fee of Rs. 10.

(b) All persons eligible to become Life Members of the

Society shall have to pay Rs. 500 per annum and an entrance fee of Rs. 10. Such persons shall be eligible to be enrolled as Life Members of the Society.

(c) The receipt shall be issued to the members on receipt of subscription amount and entrance fees, etc., and the person who received the amount shall sign the receipt.

(5) Property of the Society:

(a) All the movable and immovable property of the Society and social agencies/organisations shall be of the ownership of the SWAD Welfare Society.

(b) All the donations, subscriptions, funds and other amounts collected in the name of the Society will belong to the Society.

(6) Funds of the Society:

(a) The Society can raise its funds by way of: (1) subscriptions, (2) donations, (3) entrance fees, (4) miscellaneous receipts and fees, and (5) subsidies grants or other assistance from Indian or Foreign Governments/ agencies/organisation and individuals.

(b) By conducting charitable shows from time to time.

(c) By any other legal sources.

(d) No Member shall at any time be permitted to withdraw the subscription or donations made by him.

(e) No refund of the donations or subscriptions shall be permitted.

(f) The Board of Directors may receive deposits from members and they may frame rules regarding the receipts of such deposits, and they may change them from time to time. The interest payable on such deposits shall not ordinarily exceed 8 per cent per annum.

(7) Borrowing Funds:

The total borrowings of the Society shall not exceed 20 times its yearly subscription.

(8) Management of the Society:

The management of the Society shall vest in the Board of Directors consisting of 11 members who shall be elected/ nominated/selected from among the members through a meeting of the General Body of the Society.

(9) Disqualifications for Directorship:

The selected/nominated/elected Director of the Society shall cease to hold office if:

(a) He is interested directly or indirectly in any contract made with such Society privately or in any contract or transaction of the Society (other than investments, deposits and borrowing) involving financial interest in that contract, sale, purchase or transaction.

(b) He is working against the objectives of the Society.

(10) Executives of the Board/Society:

The following executives will be elected in the first meeting of the executive body.

(a) *President*: The President shall be elected by the Board at its first meeting and shall hold office for five years or till the date of the next elections.

(b) *Vice President*: The Vice President shall be elected by the Board at its first meeting and shall hold office for five years or till the date of next elections.

(c) *Treasurer*: The Treasurer shall be elected by the Board at its first meeting and shall hold office for five years or till the date of next elections.

(d) *Secretary and Joint Secretary*: There shall be a Secretary and Joint Secretary appointed by the board. They shall be paid such amount as honorarium as shall be decided by the Board of Directors, provided the work of the Society increases.

The President, or in his absence the Vice President, shall preside over all the meetings of the Board. In the absence of the Vice President, the Directors present shall elect a Chairman from amongst the members.

(11) Special Powers of the Executives:

(a) *President and Vice President*: The President and Vice-President of the Society will be given full powers to take decisions in certain important and confidential cases/matters of the Society or any social agency or organisation of the Society.

(b) *Treasurer*: The Treasurer shall have the power to keep minimum Rs. 1000 with him for day-to-day expenses of the Society and its social agencies and the remaining amount of the Society or social agencies will have to be deposited in the bank in the joint account of the Society only.

(12) The meeting of the Board of Directors may be convened whenever necessary, but it should be done so at least once in three months.

(13) The questions at the meeting of the Board shall be decided by a majority of votes and Chairman of the meeting shall have a second or casting vote in the event of equality of votes.

(14) Seven Directors shall form a quorum.

(15) No Director shall vote upon or take part in the discussion of any matter in which he is personally interested.

(16) Duties and Powers of the Board:
The duties of the Board are:
   (a) To maintain all the accounts and registers prescribed under the Rules and Act or prescribed by special or general orders of the concerned officers.
   (b) To convene the annual special general meetings to issue notice and the agenda of such meetings and to place before such meetings all matters required as per the bylaws of the Society.
   (c) To arrange for the inspection of the agencies/ organisations/institutions started by the Society and also the moveable and immovable properties of the Society.

(17) Powers of the Board:
   (a) To raise or borrow money required for the purpose of the Society and its Institutions from any of the cooperative banks, industrial banks, nationalised banks or any legal source.
   (b) To appoint employees/officers and to fix wages or salaries to be paid to each employee and also to take disciplinary actions against any misconduct of such employees.
   (c) To appoint the paid Executive Director of the Society for the administration and management of the Society and all the social agencies/organisations of the Society.
   (d) To exercise all such powers, enter into any agreements, make all such arrangements, take all such proceedings, do all such acts, and things as may be necessary and proper for management and administration of the affairs of the Society and for carrying out the objects of the

Society and for securing and furthering its interests.

(e) To frame rules as are necessary from time to time for conducting the business or starting different social agencies/organisations/institutions of the Society as are consistent with the Act, the Rules and their bylaws, subject to the approval of the Registrar of the societies concerned.

(f) To fix up the day and date of the election and method of election.

(g) To open joint account in any bank in the name of the President, Vice President and Secretary or Executive Director (any two members' signatures will be necessary for the purpose.

(18) The Board shall have to record the minutes of the meetings in the books meant for the purpose in respect of the following matters:

(a) The names of members of the Board present at each meeting of the Board.

(b) The proceedings of all meetings of the Board and of the executives or committees and sub-committees.

(c) The Proceedings of all General Meetings: The minutes of the Board and other committee meetings shall be confirmed at the next meeting of the Board. The minutes of the General meeting shall be confirmed and signed by the Chairman of the Board at the next meeting of the Board, such confirmed minutes for all purposes whatsoever be the *prima facie* evidence of the matters contained therein.

(19) No acts done in good faith by the Board shall be held to be invalid merely by reasons of any defect in the constitution of the Board or in the appointment of any Member thereof.

(20) The Board shall be competent to constitute a sub-committee and/or committees and also to delegate all or any of the powers to such committees or sub-committees.

(21) Powers of the Officers:

The several officers of the society shall have the powers mentioned below subject to such resolutions as the Board may pass from time to time.

(a) The Secretary/Executive Director shall be the custodian of all the records of Society and shall be responsible for the correct and up-to-date maintenance of the accounts of the Society.

(b) The Secretary/Executive Director shall be responsible for the management and administration of the Society subject to the control of the President. The President shall execute all bonds of the Society and another Director authorised by the board and Secretary/Executive Director. The Secretary/Executive Director shall sign cash book in the token of its correctness and shall be competent to incur contingent expenditure subject to a maximum of Rs. 50 for any item as may be fixed by the Board from time to time. The Secretary/Executive Director shall in consultation with the President convene the meeting of the Board. He shall attend all meetings of the society and the Board and record the minutes of their proceedings and do such other work as may be entrusted to him. In the absence of the Secretary/Executive Director the Chairman of the meeting may require any member of the Board/establishment to record the said minutes.

(c) The Secretary/Executive Director, and in case of any temporary emergency, other officer of the Society authorised by the President and the Vicepresident shall jointly have powers for and on behalf of the Society to operate all the banking accounts of the Society. The Secretary/ Executive shall endorse transfer of any promissory notes, Government and other Securities, or foreign governments or organisation's instruments standing in the name of or held by the Society, and sign, endorse and negotiate cheques and other negotiable instruments and sign all receipts and accounts and other documents connected with the business of social agencies of the Society. The Secretary/Executive Director or any other official ordered by the President shall take the cash balance at the close of each day.

(22) The society shall, within a period of three months after the date fixed for making up its accounts for the year under rules,

call for a general meeting of its members.

(23) The special general meeting of the Society may be called at any time by a resolution of the Board and shall be called within one month of the receipt of a requisition in writing, stating the purpose for which the meeting is to be called from....

- (a) one-third of the members of the Society or 20, whichever is less, or,
- (b) The Registrar of the Societies concerned.

(24) At least 15 days clear notice shall be given to the members for convening a meeting of the General Body and 21 days clear notice for calling the Special General Meeting. The subjects not included in the Agenda cannot be discussed at the meeting unless two third of the members present are in favour of it. The question of removal of the members from the register of members or amending of bylaws shall not be discussed at any meeting unless it is specified in the notice convening the meetings.

(25) The General Body of the Society shall be the causing of the members of the Society and organisation including the Directors of the Board.

(26) Functions of the General Body Meeting:
The general body meeting shall, among other things deal with the following matters:

- (a) Receive the Board, the balance sheet and the report for the preceding year,
- (b) Consider the audit report and expenditure reports,
- (c) Elect the Directors subject to the bylaws,
- (d) Consider amendment to the bylaws,
- (e) Consider the removal of any member under bylaws,
- (f) Consider complaints which any member may refer gainst the Board,
- (g) Consider any other matter of which the notice has been given, and
- (h) Appoint the replacement/co-opting of the executive member of the Board.

(27) Election of the Members to the Board of Director shall be conducted in accordance with the rules made under the Act in force.

(28) The President of the Board of Directors or in his absence the Vice President or in his absence any member chosen by the members present shall preside over the General Meeting. All questions/matters shall be decided by a majority of votes of the members present and voting, when votes have a casting vote, except in election of members of the committee.

(29) The quorum at the General Body Meeting or at the Special General Meeting called under bylaws shall be one-fifth of the total membership or 20, whichever is less.

(30) Use of the Funds of the Society:
The funds of the Society shall be used for the purpose of attaining the objectives and goals of the Society, subject to the rules as may be framed by the Board from time to time in consultation with the advisory committee of the Society.

(31) Profits:
From the gross income, interest paid and payable on the borrowings, all sums paid and payable on account of costs of management and all other sums chargeable to Profit and Loss account for the year for which the accounts are to be made up under the rules shall be deducted and the balance remaining shall be treated as net profits. And all sums realised in respect of fines, entrance fees, etc., variations in the Provisions of this bylaws can be made by resolution of the General Body Meeting and with all sanction of the Registrar concerned.

(32) Reserve Funds: Disposal of Reserve Funds:
The whole reserve fund of the Society is kept to meet the unforeseen losses. It shall be invested only in the District Central Co-operative bank and shall not be drawn upon except with the Permission of the Registrar of the Societies concerned/Director Social Welfare (State or Central).

(33) Amendments of Bylaws:
Subject to the rules, bylaws can be amended provided that notice of the amendment has been given to the members at least 15 days before the date of the General Body Meeting. The Amendments shall take effect only if they are approved and registered under the Societies Registration Act, 1960, and Rules, 1961.

(34) Balance Sheet:
Within one month after the close of the year on 31st March for with the accounts are to be made up according to the Rules, the Board shall draw up the statements showing receipts and disbursement, assets and liabilities, profits and loss and such other returns as the Registrar concerned may prescribe from time to time and submit a copy of each of such statements and returns to the Registrar of Societies, Director of Social Welfare (State or/and Central) concerned.

(35) No amendments to alteration in or cancellation of bylaws or the amendment of new bylaws shall be made except at a General meeting or shall be given effect to until it is approved and registered by the Registrar concerned.

(36) The provisions of the Registration of the Societies Act, 1960, and the rules framed thereunder shall be deemed to be part of these bylaws.

(37) In the case of any doubt regarding the construction or interpretation of an Act, the rules thereunder of the Bylaws or in regard to any other matter, the Board of Directors shall obtain the advice of the Registrar concerned and abide by it.

Certificate

This is to certify that the copies of the rules and regulations of the Trust/Society, i.e., ____________________ are true and original.

Sr. No.	*Directors/Officers Names*	*Designation*	*Signature*
1.			
2.			
3.			
4.			
5.			

Place:
Date:

Letter of Exemption

To,
Hon'ble Deputy Charity Commissioner
_________________ Division,
____

Sub:
Request for exemption from publishing notice in the newspaper.

Sir,

We have submitted an application for registration of our Trust/Society under the rules of Public Trust Act, 1952. The said Trust/Society is newly established by us and it has no moveable or immovable property. Hence, we may kindly be exempted from publishing a notice in the Newspaper under Section 7a.

Thanking you,

Yours faithfully,

____
Secretary
Place:
Date:

Request of Registration

To,
Hon'ble Deputy Charity Commissioner
_________________ Division,
Office of the Charity Commission,
____

Sub: Request for registration of our Trust/Society under the Public Trust Act, 1952, and The Societies Registration Act, 1960.

Sir,

With reference to the above cited subject we write to inform you that all the required documents are attached with the original application submitted for the registration of our Trust/Society on _____________________ and we have no other document or explanation to be submitted as an evidence for registration. You are, therefore, requested to register our Trust/Society and oblige.

Thanking you,

Yours faithfully,

____

Secretary
Place:
Date:

Consent Letter

To,
Hon'ble Deputy Charity Commissioner
__________________ Division,
Office of the Charity Commission,
__________________ Division,
____

Sir,

Mr. __________________, Secretary, ________________________ has submitted an application for registration of our Trust/Society under the Public Trust Act, 1952 and the Societies Registration Act, 1860, on __________________ along with the required documents. In this connection we write to inform you that the information given in the application is true and there is no other say of the Board in this regard and it is not necessary to issue us a separate notice of hearing regarding registration. Hence, we have no objection to issuance of a certificate of registration to him.

Yours faithfully,

Name of the Trustee　　　　　Signature
(i) Mr./Mrs. __________________
(ii)
(iii)
(iv)

(v)
(vi)
(vii)

Place:
Date:

Name and Signature of the Applicant

Witness: The above persons and their signatures are known to me

Letter Regarding Use of Certificate

To,
Hon'ble Deputy Charity Commissioner
________________ Division,
Office of the Charity Commission,
_______________ Division,
____

Sub: Regarding use of Registration Certificate

Sir,

With reference to the above cited subject, we, the members and executives of our Trust/Society, write to inform you that after registration of our Trust/Society under the rules of Public Trust Act, 1952, and The Societies Registration Act, 1860, a certificate of registration issued to us will not be used for running drawing lottery, and for such other reasons which will be in contravention to the objectives and goals of the Organisation.

Yours faithfully,

Name of the Trustee Signature

(i) Mr./Mrs. _________________
(ii)
(iii)
(iv)
(v)

(vi)
(vii)

Place: Secretary
Date:

____
____

Schedule 2

The information of the employees appointed by the Trust/Society upto 31st March, 2000.

Sr. No.	*Name of the Employee*	*Minimum Pay Scale*	*Part Time/ Temporary /Perma-nent*	*Monthly Basic*	*Dearness Allowance*	*Special Pay*	*Other Allowances*	*PF*

President Vice President Secretary Treasurer

Schedule-6 Sec Rule 15

(i) Name of the Trust/Society
(ii) Registration No

Sr. No.	*Full Name of Member and Address*	*Date of Joining of the Member*	*Signature*	*Remarks*

President Vice President Secretary Treasurer

Schedule D
Consent Letter

To,
Hon'ble Deputy Charity Commissioner
________________ Division,
Office of the Charity Commission,
______________ Division,
____

Sub: Consent of the Directors to work according to the objectives and rules and regulations of the Trust/Society

Sir,

We, the Members and Directors of ____________________, hereby declare and give our consent to the concerned authorities, that we will work according to the objectives, goals and rules and regulations of the Trust/Society. Hence, the application submitted in your office for the registration may be considered and our Trust/Society be registered and oblige. We have signed here below as representative of the society.

S. No.	*Name of the Members and Directors*	*Signature*

Witness: We recognise the above persons and their signatures
(i) (ii) Seal
Special Magistrate/Advocate Secretary

Schedule E
Authority Letter

To,
Hon'ble Deputy Charity Commissioner
________________ Division,
Office of the Charity Commission,
________________ Division,

____

Sub:
Authority to change the documents of registration if the needs arises

Sir,

We, the Members and Executives of ________________, hereby authorise Mr. ________________, Secretary of the Trust/Society, to make any alterations or changes in the original documents submitted in your office for registration.

Sr. No.	*Name of the Member Executive*	*Signature*

Place:
Date:

Authorised Person is

Note: Authority letter given to me by the Board accepted for the purpose.

Covering Letter

To,
Hon'ble Executive Magistrate,
TQ____________ Dist.

Sub: Request to complete the affidavit, enclosed with the application.

Sir,

Please find enclosed herewith an affidavit on stamp paper worth Rs. 10 in connection with the registration of our Trust/Society, i.e., ____________, and please do the needful in this regard and extend your cooperation for completing the process of registration of the above mentioned Trust in the office of the Charity Commission.

Thanking you,

Yours Faithfully,

____

Place:
Date:
Affix Court fee stamp Rs. 1.

Schedule F
Affidavit

To,
Hon'ble Executive Magistrate,
TQ___________ Dist.

Before ________________

I, the undersigned ___________, Secretary ___________, aged ________________, occupation ________________, reside at ____________.

I am a Member and Executive of ____________________, and am going to submit an application in the office of the Charity Commission for registration under the Public Trust Act, 1952, and the Societies Registration Act, 1960, on ________, and I hereby make a statement that all the information mentioned in the constitution of the above Trust/Society and all other documents are true and correct. The said Trust/Society is formed to render the social services for the poor, needy and sufferers in different communities.

I also say and make a statement that I recognise all the members and executives of the Trust/Society, and till today no change has taken place in the documents of the society.

I say and make a statement that no other Society/Trust is in existence by this name or similar to this in our village.

I say and make a statement that till this date this Trust/Society does not have any moveable or immovable property, except the cash/amount Rs. ____ which is with me in the name of Organisation.

I say and make a statement that the address of the Trust/Society and address given for communication by belongs to one Shri ________________ and it is in his/her possession. An authenticated document, i.e., true copy of the extract and statement is enclosed herewith for your information and record and I, and all other members will be responsible if there is any change or dispute in this regard. I will also inform you of any change address of communications. The official communication to you is my responsibility.

Date ___________

Witness

Sd Addresses

(i)

(ii)

Court fee Stamp Worth Rs. 2.

Establishment of NGO and Functions

The procedure laid down by the concerned department, which is described for learning gives an idea to the trainee students in setting up voluntary organisations and the procedural knowledge enhances their confidence to do it. But they should understand the significance for establishing them from the point of view of making use of their professional training to do social work practice for the needy, poor and sufferers. Moreover, establishing NGOs on their own will enhance their practical knowledge, social perspective and outlook of work. It builds up their professional career and it will be useful in guiding youngsters to set up voluntary organisations. The students should however bear in mind that merely learning the procedure of setting up a voluntary organisation is not enough to guide others. They should also know how to run the organisation.

After registration, for the first two years grants are not given to the NGOs either by governmental or by non-governmental funding agencies and without funds it is not possible for the students to run the organisation. Hence, they should think of ideas and techniques to carry on the functions without money/funds.

Initially, students should chalk out small programmes on the basis of the objectives and goals of the organisation during the period of training in the summer vacation. For example, (i) essay competitions, (ii) elocution competitions, (iii) drawing competitions, (iv) exhibitions of posters, (v) organisation of sports, (vi) organisation of dance competitions, (vii) singing competitions, (viii) organisation of healthy child competitions, (ix) organisation of eye camps, (x) organisations of guest lectures, (xi) organisation of hobby classes, (xii) organisation of cultural programmes, and (xiii) organisation of guidance services and such other useful functions.

To conduct small activities, the student founders can prepare a plan on plain paper and approach concerned institutions. For example, they can approach high schools for conducting essay competitions and seek their formal permission to display the notices on their notice boards for the information of the children. Such notices will definitely motivate those children to participate in the function to win the competitions and progress. The student founders or organisers should frame the rules and regulations of the competitions. A small subscription can be kept for participation. Similarly, the prizes or funds can be collected from different sources in the communities, i.e., the wealthy, friends, officers, etc. This public fund can be utilised for organising the function of prize distribution. Any renowned person who is easily available can be invited to be the chief guest of the function. The distribution of prizes at the hands of such renowned persons assists the organisers and the organisation to earn name and fame. The news of such functions should also be drafted immediately and sent to the newspapers for publication. The published news cuttings should be collected for maintaining the records of the organisation. In this way the resources of the communities can be utilised to do social activities for two years and render services.

After two years the newly established organisation becomes eligible for getting grants from governmental as well as non-governmental organisations. To make the procedure easy the founders can contact organisations like SOSVA, Pune. SOSVA is an NGO, which imparts training to the voluntary workers or trained social workers of any NGO or GO and assists them to prepare proposals of grants-in-aid and guides them in the procedure for getting grants. It is to be noted that SOSVA also renders consultancy services for getting grants to any NGO. For this, the founders can contact the concerned officers of SOSVA to collect detailed information and procedures. Similarly, they can collect information from them as regards name and addresses of the funding agencies, formats of the proposals, application forms, government schemes, i.e., state government schemes, central government schemes, private funding organisations and their schemes, national and international funding agencies, etc. Collection of such information and office procedures will definitely pave way to build up a professional career in social work.

Think and Do

"Complete your summer training in setting up an NGO by registering your own organisation and start practising social work through it whenever you find the time. By the time you complete your MSW course your organisation becomes a year old and then it becomes easy to march ahead and get funds from government or private funding agencies."

Bibliography

Bet, V.P., *Note on Field Instructions*, TAPASWEE, Avanti Nagar, Solapur, Maharashtra, 1989.

Delhi School of Social Work, *Fieldwork Supervision*, Delhi University, Delhi, 1957.

Jacob, K.K., *Fifty Years of Social Work Education in India.*

Lawani, B.T., "A Critical Study of Fieldwork Training in Social Work Education in Shivaji University", Kolhapur (unpublished M. Phil Dissertation), 1989.

MASWE, *Sixty Years of Social Work Education*, Nagpur, 1995.

Murthy, M.V. and S.N. Rao, *Fieldwork and Social Work*, Waltair, Department, of Sociology and Social Work, 1970.

Pathak, Bindeshwar, *Continuity and Change in Indian Society*, Concept Publishing Company, New Delhi, 1998.

Pathan, K.G. and B.T. Lawani, *Fieldwork Training in Social Work Education*, Bharati Vidyapeeth, Bijapur Road, Solapur, Maharashtra, 1990.

Singh, *R.R., Fieldwork in Social Work Education* (A Perspective for Human Services Profession), Concept Publication Co., New Delhi, 1985.

Srinivas, M.N., *The Fieldworkers and the Field*, Delhi, Oxford University Press, 1983.

Subhedar, I.S., Note on Fieldwork Training in Social Work, SWASS, 7, Namrata Appt. Kadamwadi Road, Maharashtra, 1988.

Index

agency supervision
  methods of, 47-48
agency supervisors
  functions of, 45-46
  problems faced by, 50-51

casework diary, 84-87
  purposes of maintaining a, 36
casework training, 71
  objectives of, 71
casework, 70
  evaluation of, 81
  procedure of, 75-80
community work
  journal writing for, 136-37
  recording diary for, 133-36

Delhi School of Social Work, 25, 27, 33, 201
Dewey, 23

faculty supervision
  methods of, 46-47
faculty supervisors
  functions of, 43-44
  – during the various phases, 44-45
  problems faced by, 49-50
fieldwork
  components of, 30
  concept of, 22-23
  curriculum of, 26-30
  definitions of, 24
  nature and structure of, 32
  objectives of, 24-26
  problems in, 30-32, 70
  procedure of, 120
  recording information during the, 36-37
  supervision of, 33-36, 39-56
  through films, 192-97
  – advantages of, 195-97
fieldwork evaluation, 198
  definitions of, 199
  objectives of, 199-200
  patterns of, 200
  process of, 200-1
fieldwork supervision, 33, 39
  definition of, 40
  methods of, 34-36
  objectives of, 42
  phases of, 33-34
  problems in, 48-53
  – relating to: students, 49; faculty supervisors, 49-50; agency supervisors, 50-51;

fieldwork supervision
  agencies, 51-52; schools, 52-53
fieldwork supervisor
  roles of, 33-34
fieldwork training, 26-27
  components of, 30
  in community organisations, 117, 126-30
  – objectives of, 118-19
  phases of, 27-29
  – contents of, 27-29
films
  on social issues, 196-97

Garrette, Annette, 23
group work diary, 110-11
group work journal, 111-12
group work practice, 99
group work programme
  planning for, 97-99
group work recordings, 109-16
group work training, 95
objectives of, 96
group work, 95
components of, 99-108

journal writing, 36, 87-94

lagori
  game of, 114-16
  – rules of, 115-16

NGO
  functions of, 270
  setting up an, 239-41

orientation training, 57
  evaluation of, 68-69
  methods of, 58-59
  objectives of, 57-58
  procedure of, 59-61

Richmond, Mary, 22
rural social work camp(s), 157
  and rural social service camp(s), 156
  – difference between, 157, 158-60
  objectives of, 157-58
  preliminary preparations for, 164-68

sanskar programmes, 102
Schmidt and Perry, 199
schools of social work
  in India
  – for effective supervision, needs of the, 53-54
  – problems faced by, 30-32; school-specific, 31; agency-specific, 31; student-specific, 32
self-evaluation, 83-84, 132-33
self-study
  methods of, 72-74, 119-20
social functions, 138
  participation in
  – benefits of, 144
  – objectives of, 138-39
social work education
  fieldwork in, 22, 24
  – components of, 30
  – objectives of, 25
  in India, 235

social work education
  origin of, 22, 235
  supervision in, 40, 41
  – concept of, 40
social work supervision
  aims of, 41
  aspects of, 41-42
  functions of, 41
study tour(s), 145-46
  methods of training during, 148
  objectives of, 146-47
  organisation of, 148-50
  syllabus for, 147-48
Subhedar, Iqbal, 199
summer training, 236
  curriculum of, 237-38
  objectives of, 236-37
  process of, 238
supervision
  characteristic of, 39
  definitions of, 39-40
  functions of, 39, 41
  meaning of, 39

Tata Institute of Social Sciences, 13
Terry, George R., 39
Towle, 40